The Lowrie

As acted in part by Henry Berry Lowrie,
the great North Carolina bandit, with
biographical sketch of his associates

Mary C. Norment,

Fred A. Olds

Alpha Editions

This edition published in 2020

ISBN : 9789354042942

Design and Setting By
Alpha Editions
www.alphaedis.com
email - alphaedis@gmail.com

THE
Lowrie
History

AS ACTED IN PART BY

Henry Berry
..LOWRIE..

THE LOWRIE HISTORY

AS ACTED IN PART BY

Henry Berry Lowrie,

THE

Great North Carolina Bandit,

WITH BIOGRAPHICAL SKETCH OF

HIS ASSOCIATES.

ILLUSTRATED.

Being a Complete History of the Modern Robber Band in the County
of Robeson and State of North Carolina.

WITH AN APPENDIX.

PUBLISHED BY
LUMBEE PUBLISHING COMPANY,
LUMBERTON, N. C.

INTRODUCTORY

In re-publishing this book which records the events of a period of Robeson county's history in the years of 1864-'74, the publishers have thought it fitting and proper, in justice to the race of people, (some of whose representatives figure in and are the leading characters of the facts recorded), that a supplement should be added, showing the growth and steady improvement of the Indians of Robeson County, and to accomplish this desired end we do not know of anything better than to copy, in part, an article written by Col. A. F. Olds, of Raleigh, N. C., who visited this saction of Robeson County and came in personal touch with the Croatan Indians, and has therefore written from personal observation. We are therefore indebted to Col. Olds for this interesting bit of history, which forms the appendix to this volume.

It will be remembered that the facts recorded in this book were written by one who knew the cause and result of this unfortunate period of Robeson's history, having lived "through the thick or the fight", and gained the information recorded by actual experience. The historian referred to is Mrs. Mary C. Norment, of Elrod, N. C., from whom the copy-right of this book has been purchased by the publishers.

This is the fourth edition of this history.

THE PUBLISHERS.

The Lowrie History.

James Lowrie, a tall well-proportioned, fine looking, respectable Indian first settled in Robeson county about the year 1769. This was Bladen county at that time. On the 9th of August, 1769, James Lowrie bought a tract of land containing one hundred acres from William Fort, to whom it was granted by George II. in 1748. He also entered another tract of land containing three hundred acres adjoining the above tract, the grant being signed by George III. On the above mentioned tracts of land, now owned by the heirs of the late Col. Archibald McEachern, James Lowrie first settled.

About five hundred yards below the residence of Col. McEachern, in a bend of the swamp, is shown the place where James Lowrie resided. McPhaul's mills, on the same swamp, are distant about three miles. This swamp was called Lowrie Swamp, after James Lowrie, who resided on it. A ford at the time he lived there crossed the swamp at his residence. Here he raised stock, farmed in a small way and kept a tavern during the Revolutionary War. James Lowrie first came to Robeson (then Bladen county) from Bute county, (now Franklin and Warren counties) in company with Silas Atkins, who emigrated also from Bute county, from that portion now called Franklin. Other families also, viz. the Thompsons, Kitchens Coles, Drakes, Moores, Humphreys, Bridgers, and whose descendants still live in Robeson,

came to Bladen county, (now Robeson) from that part
of North Carolina embraced now in the counties of
Franklin, Warren, Nash and Edgecombe and settled
here about the time that Silas Atkins first built on the
tract of land now owned by William H. Graham.

James Lowrie, from whom all the Lowries in Robeson descended, lived in Franklin county before he emigrated to Robeson. It was in Franklin county, N. C.,
that he was manumitted by his father, James Lowrie,
of Virginia, who when Virginia became one of the
United States, was elected a Judge, and was ever afterwards known as Judge Lowrie. He was of cavalier
stock and characterized by elegance and refinement of
manners, tall and commanding in personal appearance,
urbane, courtly and genteel in his whole deportment.
It was in Franklin county that James Lowrie married.
His wife's maiden name was Sarah Kearsey, (nicknamed
Sally Kearsy,) a half-breed Tuscarora Indian woman,
and from this couple all the Lowries in Robeson trace
back their origin.

The above statement in regard to the origin of the
Lowrie family in Robeson county is not current rumor,
but a true statement, as given by James Lowrie himself and corroborated by Silas Atkins, with whom he
came to Robeson county in 1769, also confirmed by the
late Neil Brown, Esq., who lived on Richland Swamp;
by the late Mrs. Nancy Smith, mother of Rev. A.Smith,
who also lived on Richland Swamp; by the late Sampson Bridgers, father of J. D. Bridgers, Esq., by Henry
Thompson; by Nathan Thompson; by John Thompson,
by Peter Monroe, and last, though not least, by the late
John Gilchrist, Esq., long a practicing lawyer at the

Lumberton Bar, whose father bought out James Lowrie
in 1791, at the close of the Revolutionary War.

James Lowrie had three sons, viz: William, Thomas
and James, and at the commencement of the Revolutionary War William, his oldest, being then about
grown, entered into the struggle for independence and
joined the brave and patriotic band, then under the
command of that noble Whig patriot, Col. Thomas Robeson, after whom and in honor of whom Robeson county was named. William Lowrie made a good Whig
soldier and fought side by side with the whites in every
skirmish and battle in which Col. Robeson was engaged.
Whilst piloting Col. Wade and his men across Drowning
Creek, after a massacre at Piney Bottom, in Cumberland county, William Lowrie received a severe sword
cut in his left hand from a Tory named James McPher-
son, who resided on the place then owned by Col.
Charles Malloy, now Laurel Hill Church, in Richmond
county.

The skirmish between Col. Wade's men and the Tories took place on the spot of ground on which Mont-
pelier Church was erected, near Bettie's bridge, now
Gilchrist's bridge, in the upper portion of Robeson county, immediately on Drowning Creek, in Robeson county, and William Lowrie carried the marks of this wound
to his grave as a token of his devotion to the Whig
cause. After the close of the Revolutionary War William Lowrie received a pension for this same sword cut
from the government up to the day of his death, as the
records in the Pension Office at Washington City will
show.

The other two sons of James Lowrie, viz: Thomas
and James, were of tender age and too young to enter

the service. The feelings and sentiments of James
Lowie, their father, were on the Whig side, although he
took no active part either way. Living, however, so
near to McPhaul's Mill, (a distance of not more than
three miles) the then general rendezvous or head-quar-
ters of the Tories from the whole adjacent country, he
became obnoxious to them on account of his son William being in the Whig ranks.

Soon after the close of the Revolutionary War, pre-
judices becoming so rife against him and his son William, on account of Whig principles, James Lowrie
sold out on Lowrie Swamp to John Gilchrist in
1791, and moved down on Drowning Creek, near his
old friend Silas Atkins and settled on the place now
known as "the Harper Ferry place." Here he kept a
house of entertainment for the traveling public, in connection with a grocery or drinking saloon. Here he
died, leaving land and negroes to his children and a
good name to his posterity. Here, in Lowrie's grocery,
Col. Vick, then merchandising at Fair Bluff, in Robeson county. (Vicksburg in Mississippi being named after
him) christened (to use a scotch phrase) all that region
lying East of Drowing Creek and extending one or two
Miles East of Bear Swamp with the euphonious soubriquet
of Scuffletown, from the fact of the half breeds inhabit-
ing that region congregating in Lowrie's grocery and
after imbibing pretty freely of whiskey, in engaging in
the broad shuffle, and also from the fact that it was
generally a scuffle with these people to live—"to keep
the soul and body together," owing to their improvident
habits. After the death of James Lowrie, his son William Lowrie married Bettie Locklaer, a half-breed
Tuscarora Indian woman(Locklaer meaning "hold fast").

Thomas Lowrie, his second son, married Nancy Deas,
a white woman. James Lowrie, his third son, never
married. Allen Lowrie, a son of William Lowrie, married Pollie Cumba, a woman of Portuguese extraction.
He raised a large family of sons and daughters; and four
of his sons, viz: William Lowrie, Steve Lowrie, Thomas
Lowrie, Henry Berry Lowrie, were concerned in the
depredations committed in the county of Robeson, from
their inception, while it is due to history to record that
his other sons had no connection whatever with their
four brothers engaged in robbing. Henry Berry Lowrie,
one of the younger brothers, assumed the command of
the Robber Band and was styled Chief.   Two other
members of the Robber Band, viz: Calvin and Henderson Oxendine, lineally descended from the Lowrie family, on the mother's side.   Boss and Andrew Strong,
two other members of the band, and Lowrie blood
coursing their veins, their mother being of the Lowrie
stock; their father, John Strong was a white man, who
come into Robeson county and settled in Scuffletown. An accident connected with the history of John
Strong was related to the writer several years ago.
At the Fall Term of the Superior Court of Robeson in
1843, John B. Kelly, Esq., of Moore county, then a
practicing Lawyer at the Lumberton Bar, meet up with
John Strong, whom he knew personally, and addressed
him as Gorman. Strong replied and said his name was
Strong.   John B. Kelly replied and told him to be off,
for he wns a villian.   Having killed a man in Alamance
county, he fled to Robeson to save his neck and assumed the name of Strong, but his real name was Gorman.
Two other members of the Robber Band, viz: William
Chavis and George Applewhite, (formerly a slave,)were

connected with the Lowrie family by marriage. The
only members of the Robber gang that were not con-
nected with the Lowrie family by affinity or consan-
guinity, were Zach T. McLauchlin, a low-bred youth of
Scottish descent, Shoemaker John, a negro and William
Chavis, a bright half-breed Indian. These Henry Berry Lowrie, Chief; Stephen Lowrie, William Lowrie,
Thomas Lowrie, Calvin Oxendine, Henderson Oedine,
Boss Strong, Andrew Strong, William Chavis, George
Applewhite, being all kinfolk, together with Zach T.
McLauchlin, Shoemaker John, and William Chavis,
were concerned all of them, in robberies, murders, and
depredations committed in the county of Robeson, from
the latter part of the year, A. D., 1864, to February
24th, A. D. 1874.

DESCRIPTION OF THE LOWRIE ROBBERS.

Pen and ink sketches of personages convey very often
but faint ideas of individuals, although they may be correct in every particular. It is very difficult to impress
most minds with distinct ideas of things without presen-
tation of the object to the eyes, they being the mirrow,
as it were, that reflect images on the mental vision.
However, we will attempt a description of the Lowrie
Bandits, for the benefit of those who have never seen
them:

HENRY BERRY LOWRIE, THE LEADER OF THE BAND.

Henry Berry Lowrie, the leader of the band, is a son
of Allen Lowrie, and a great grand-son of James Lowrie, from whom all the the Lowries in Robeson descended. He is of mixed blood, strangely commingled, hav-

ing coursing his veins the blood of the Tuscarora Indian, and the Cavalier blood of England.   He made a
handsome personal appearance when dressed up   The
color of his skin is of a mixed white and yellow, par-
taking of an admixture, resembling copper, the Indian
color however, still predominating.   Such a skin is affected very little by heat or cold, by sickness or health,
or by exposure. or good housing.   A scar in the shape
of a crescent and of a blackish color is on his face just
below his left eye, said to have been made by an iron
pot falling on him when a child.   The contour of his
face is that of a Southron.   His countenance is ex-
pressive in the highest degree of firmness, decision of
character and courage.   Generally he is reticent, a
good listener, seldom talkative, manifesting in his demeanor little or no disposition at self importance. When
he converses, he talks like an illiterate man, conversant
with no books except of nature, and human nature.
Considering his long career of lawlessness, his want of
education and his race, he is a prodigy. Phrenologi-
cally speaking, his forehead is good, high, broad and
massive; the color of his eyes is a grayish hazel, and
when excited and agitated, would dilate and expand.
A smile generally played over his countenance when quiet
but when aroused it was a smile of a demon.   He wore a
dark goatee, his hair was straight and black like an Indian's.
He was twenty-six years old, five feet ten inches high,
and weighs about one hundred and fifty pounds. Physi-
cally he was well knit, straight in the back, his arms and
shoulders fitting on well, a deep broad chest; in short,
proportioned throughout without a flaw in his frame.
Like an india rubber ball, he was elastic all over.   In

his dress he was rather careless and negligent. He generally wore calf-skin boots, a woolen frock coat or blouse, breeches or trousers of the same material, mostly, however, of Salem or Kentucky Jeans, with a wide brimmed felt hat. Although a tippler, he was never known to be intoxicated, he invariably carried a flask of whiskey with him wheresoever he went. He did this to avoid being poisoned by promiscuous drinking.

In regard to his arms: a belt around his waist kept in place five six barrelled revolvers long shooters; from this belt a shoulder strap passes up and supports behind, slinging style, a Henry rifle, which carries the extraordinary number of sixteen cartridges. In addition to these fifty-two charges, he carried a long bladed knife and a double-barrelled shot gun, his whole equipment weighing not less than eighty pounds. His main object in thus equipping himself was doubtless to stand a long campaign, or to be ready with almost an arsenal at at his command, to encounter a large body of men in pursuit of him. With all his armor on he could run, swim, stand weeks of exposure in the swamps, walk day and night and take sleep by little snatches, which in a few days would tire out white or negro. Being fond of blood he has waged for the past ten years a savage predatory warfare against the county, State, Confederate and United States authority. Without advantages other than nature gave him, without fear, without hope, defying society, he carried out his tactics in a peculiar way, impressing the whole population with his superiority, power and influence as a brigand leader and executive spirit. Occasionally his blood and inclinations will crop out, and two natures of white and

Indian will come forward and show themselves to the
close observer, and in a way unlooked for. He plays
on banjo, together with the Juba beating and dancing
of the Indian girls, has on several occasions come very
near betraying him to his pursurers. His Indian nature
may be traced in his character, by his using women as
an auxilliary to war and plunder. He himself is the
Don Juan of Scuffletown. Women have been employed to betray him, but they either repent or he discovers
their purpose. He sleeps on his arms and never seems
tired; ever active, ever vigilent, he is never taken by
surprise. His cavalier scrupulousness may also be observed in the matter of a promise or a treaty. Those
most robbed and outraged by this bandit give him credit
for complying strictly to his word. Like the rattle-
snake, he generally warned before he stuck. Two
things he has never done--he has never commited arson,
nor offered to insult white females. In these two things
may be traced his cavalier blood.

The price offerd ($10.000) for his capture by the con-
stituted authorities of the State is probably the greatest
that has ever been offered for any offender of common
law—any criminal or outlaw in American history since
Jefferson Davis' fight; and why should it not be? for
Henry Berry Lowrie, the Robber Chief, has made a
personal and bloody campaign against society, longer
than the whole Revolutionary war, killing sometimes
for plunder, revenge, or defense, refusing to trust any,
even those of his own color, except those who, like himself, had shed innocent blood and put themselves out of
the path of society. In this way he collected a pack of
murderers, whom he commanded with absolute sway.

He also arrogated to himself a protectorate over the interests of all the Indians in Scuffletown, which they returned by a sort of hero-worship. Cold-blooded, malignant and murderous bandit and robber he is, and blood-stained with many murders, he is without defenders.

In the twentieth year of his age he led up to the marriage alter, as his bride, Rhoda Strong, a cousin of his; a daughter of John Strong alias Gorman, deceased, said to be in her sixteenth year, and one of the handsomest and prettiest Indian girls in all Scuffletown, sartirically nick-named by some white young wag "the Queen of Scuffletown." The marriage ceremony was performed by Hector J. McLean, Esq., at the old Lowrie homestead, in the presence of Alexander Cobb, a white man a score or two of Indians, relations of the bride and bridegroom. As soon as the ceremony was through with, A. J. McNair, with a posse of men, arrested Henry Berry Lowrie as the murderer of James P. Barnes, and hurried him off to jail in Lumberton, from whence he was carried to Whiteville, in Columbus county and placed in jail there, where he was heavily ironed. Here he filed his way out of the grated iron window bars, escaped to the woods with hand cuffs on, and made his way back to his wife in Scuffletown. This was in 1866. This was the first escape ever effected by a criminal confined in the jail at Whitesville. How he came in possession of a file, no one in the confidence of the whites can tell. Again in 1868 Henry Berry Lowrie was formally committed to jail in Lumberton by B. A. Howell, Sheriff of Robeson. This time also he made his escape by frightening the jailor when he carried him his allowance of

food, with a cocked pistol in his hand. He told the
jailor to stand aside and let him pass out of the door,
threatening to kill him if he made an alarm in fifteen
minutes.   Although twice in the hands of the officers of
the law, he has never been held to answer at the bar of
justice for his many crimes.

From the day he made his escape from the jail in
Whiteville, he has led the precarious life of a hunted
man, robber and murderer, showing at all times and
under all circumstances a ferocity, insolence and premeditation frightful to behold, destructive of all order
and subversive of all good government.

Here an accident showing the insolence of this outlaw
to the civil authorities of the county will be sketched for
ths outside world, which is literally true in every particular.   When for prudential reasons the County Commissioners ordered the Sheriff of the county to arrest
Rhoda Lowrie, the wife of the outlaw chief, he, with
the whole robber band, went to Mr. John McNair's
residence, (Mr. John McNair having been robbed by
them more than a score of times), the Robber Chief
addressed Mr. McNair as follows: "Mr. McNair I want
you to gear up and go to Lumberton, where they have
put my wife in jail, for no crime but because she is my
wife.   That ain't her fault and they can't make it so.
You go to Lumberton and tell the Sheriff and County
Commissioners that if they don't let her out of jail, I'll
retaliate on the white women of Burnt Swamp Township.   Some of them shall come to the swamp, with me,
if she is kept in jail, because they can't get me."

The swamp alluded to above, was the Back Swamp,
in which the outlaw band had their secret camp, and

on the banks of which Henry Berry Lowrie had erected
a log cabin for his wife to live in.   This cabin was built
pretty much after style of the other cabins in Scuffletown, except that it had two doors, on the sides opposite
each other, a plank floor, a small window on the end
near the chimney, with a trap-door on the floor, leading into an underground passage some sixty yards in
length, which terminated in the swamp near by, through
which the Robber Chief had escaped on several occasions when surprised by his pursuers.   This cabin
now lies in ruins, being deserted, the yard covered with
tall weeds and the underground passage filled up.
Desolation seems to brood over it, and nothing but the
long, foreboding note of the ill-omended owl, when he
utters his "tuwit" near by in the swamps, break the silence of the night there.

STEVE LOWRIE.

   Steve Lowrie, when killed was in his thirty-sixth
year; he was five feet ten inches high, and would weigh
about one hundred and seventy pounds;thick set,round-
shouldered, heavy and of great muscular power, impu-
dent in manner; insolent in speech, showing the high-
way-robber and exhibiting in his personal appearance
more of the Indian brigand than any of the outlaw gang.
His hair was thick, black and straight; his moustache
thin, black and short; a mean countenance, with blackish hazel eyes, indicating the robber and murderer of
the Murrel stamp; just such a character as needed no
prevocation to prowl around the county by day and
night. He, too, is a son of Allen Lowrie, and the oldest
of the gang.   He had an insatiable love for robbery, and

possessed an imperious temper, which involved him on
one occasion in a quarrel with his younger brother, Henry Berry Lowrie, who shot him in the eye for insubordi-
nation. He had the meanest look of any of the gang,
and he was more feared by any unlucky victim that
happened to fall into the hands of the outlaws. Steve
Lowrie has been concerned in every robbery and shooting committed by the outlaw gang. He it was that
raised his gun and filled the unfortunate prisoner, John
Sanders, the detective, with a charge of buck-shot
when blindfolded and tied to a tree. For being implicated in the murder of ex-Sheriff Reuben King he was
outlawed, apprehended, confined in jail and tried as a
murderer at Whiteville Court and found guilty. His
lawyer taking an appeal to the Supreme Court, Steve
was remanded back to jail, and before his case came up
for a hearing before the Judges on the Supreme Court
Bench, made his escape and returned to his old haunts
in Scuffletown.

TOM LOWRIE.

Another member of the outlaw gang, and a brother to
Henry Berry and Steve Lowrie, was Indian-Gipsy look-
ing. Tom Lowrie, was a darker hue and exhibiting in
his countenance a more sneaking look than his brothers.
He has been described elsewhere under the caption,
"The Killing of Tom Lowrie," which the reader can see
by referring to that head. An incident not mentioned
there will be related here. When the unfortunate John
Sanders, the detective, was condemned to be killed, Tom
Lowrie plead for his life, and being unwilling to see

his blood shed, slunk away until after the affair was over.

Andrew and Boss Strong, two brothers, were also members of the robber band, and are sketched else-where. They were nearly white, their father being a white man and their grand mother a white woman. These five, viz: Henry Berry Lowrie, Chief, Steve Lowrie, Tom Lowrie, Andrew and Boss Strong consti-tuted the robber band after the general jail delivery in Wilmington.

John Dial, who turned State's evidence, was probab-ly as bad as any of the gang. He had a wart as large as a marble, directly under the left eye on the side of his nose. He had a fierce look. The other members of the gang charged him with perjury on his evidence before Court at Whiteville. He charged George Applewhite, with the killing of ex-Sheriff King. The rest of the outlaws said that it was John Dial who fired the fatal shot, with a pistol, that terminated the earthly career of that hale old citizen. It was John Dial who shot S. E. Ward in Reuben King's parlor.

Henderson Oxendine, another one of the gang, has been portrayed in the section headed "the fate of Hen-derson Oxendine," which see. Calvin Oxendine a brother of Henderson, belonged also to the gang. They are both Indians and somewhat resemble each other. Calvin had black eyes and in their searching round, are indescribable in their glare. They partake of the expression of the Bummer and of the Gypsy, furtive, plaintive, touching and at the same time repelling. They look like genius, but are not; the study of them is a mystery.

SHOEMAKER JOHN.

Shoemaker John, so named from his occupation, being a shoemaker by trade, was a negro, as black as a
crow. He possessed a round, full face, and if he were
good for anything it was stealing, being an adept in that
business. He, together with some of the followers of
Lowrie's gang, went on a robbing expedition some time
in the autumn of 1869. They first went to the house of
Mrs. Elizabeth Carlyle, on the "Saddle Tree Swamp,"
in the north-eastern part of the county. Here they
broke into the smoke-house of Mrs. Carlyle, took nearly all of her bacon and then entered her dwelling by
force and robbed it of all its valuables. From Mrs.
Carlyle's they went to the store of Messrs. Biggs &
Hodgins, at Antioch Presbyterian Church, in upper
Robeson, and with augers bored into their store and
took various articles of merchandise. They next went
to Billy Purcell's residence, a colored freeman, and took
everything from him of any value. They then went
to Flora McFarland's residence, near Blue's Bridge, in
Richmond county, and robbed her. They then pounced
on the gun shop of ex-sheriff William Buchanan, of
Richmond county, and depleted it of every gun in it.
They then wended their way back to Scuffletown, in
Robeson county with their booty. For this offense
Shoemaker John was apprehended and tried at the
March term of the Superior Court held in Robeson in
1871, and found guilty and sentenced to serve ten years
in the State's penitentiary. He appeared to be glad to
get in the penitentiary, for the Lowrie gang had threatened to kill him on sight, having utterly repudiated him
and his acts.

WILLIAM CHAVIS.

The Chavis family in Robeson claim their origin from the celebrated Cheves family of the South, Chavis being an abbreviation of the name Cheves, but this version of their origin can hardly be correct, unless it be admitted that the founder of the family in Robeson was a fugitive, many years ago, who made his escape to Scuffletown in North Carolina, and took up his abode in this settlement. Be this as it may, there are a good many of the name now in Robeson county, and among the number William Chavis has become distinguished as an outlaw. He is a tall bright, fine looking man, about thirty years of age, well built and very muscular. As soon as he was outlawed by the civil authorities in Robeson county he made his escape to Effingham county in Georgia, near Savanah, where he broke into a store, and made his way across the Savanah River into the State of South Carolina. When in Georgia he was employed by a man who owned a sawmill by the name of Foy. Since he came over into South Carolina nothing has been heard about him.

The only white man outlawed by the civil authorities of the county was Zach T. McLaughlin, who was hired by Henry Berry Lowrie, for fifty dollars to inflict the mortal wound on the lamented Owen C. Norment. This man Zach T. McLaughlin was probably the meanest specimen of the Scotch that could be found in the county. He justly merited the fate he met up with, at the hands of Henry Biggs.

One other white man, viz: Bryan Gilbert, not a native of the county, had dealings with the outlaw gang. On the day the outlaws made what is known in Robeson county as the "Brandy Raid" on Angus Leach, this George Gilbert, was along and accompanied the outlaws to Mrs. William McKay's residence, near Floral College, and being disguised, that is, blackened, was not recognized by Miss Pat McKay, nor by Mrs. William McKay. Here he played several pieces on the piano forte in Mrs. McKay's parlor. Subsequently he went with the outlaws to Mr. David Townsend's residence, on Aaron Swamp, near Asbury Church. Having gone into Mr. Townsend's yard and being discovered, Mr. Townsend opened fire on them with a double-barreled shot gun. There Bryan Gilbert was wounded and carried off by the outlaws to their secret camp in the Back Swamp, where he lingered a short time and died. Thus fell another one of the associates of the outlaws; and now as we have given an imperfect outline of these land pirates, or human moccasins, we will proceed to delineate their mode of warfare.

MODE OF WARFARE, EQUIPMENTS, &c.

A stranger, to see these outlaws armed as they appeared sometimes at Moss Neck, Eureka and Red Banks, would be surprised at the load they carried. They generally moved about armed with a Spencer rifle, two double-barreled shot guns, one of the latter and the rifle being slung from their shoulders by a leather strap, and three or four six barreled revolvers in their belts, with cartridge boxes in a heavy canvass haversack, the whole armor weighing not less than ninety or one hundred pounds. Where these outlaws

procured their improved fire-arms (breech-loading guns)
remains to this day a mystery, but they had them and
knew how to use them.

In regard to their mode of warfare, it may be stated
that they seldom went about at night, except when they
wished to commit robberies; they would then take advantage of the darkness to put their adversary to a dis-
advantage, slip up and arrest a whole family before
they would be discovered, and then plunder at their
leisure. They generally slept at night in the cabins of
their relatives and well-wishers and befrienders. Seldom were they exposed to inclemencies of the weather
or night air; every negro and every Indian in Robeson
county would befriend them and share with them their
last morsel of bread and meat.

When they wished to put one of their enemies—one
who was hunting them—out of the way, they would go
and make a blind or two on the road or path he was expected to travel, and get in this blind, and remain there
until their victim would come along, then fire on him
without even halting him, killing him without a moment's warning. They were such adepts in construct-
ing blinds that the traveler along the road, unless his attention had been called to these blinds by one who
understood them, would pass them by unnoticed.

It was by ambuscading that they succeeded in killing
J. Brantley Harris, James P. Barnes, Owen C. Nor-
ment, Murdoch A. McLean and his brother Hugh, John
Taylor, Archibald A. McMillan, Hector McNeill,
Alexander Brown, Col. F. M. Wishart and Giles Inn-
man. All these most excellent citizens of Robeson county

met their sad fate at the hands of these modern Robeson
county Apaches—these North Carolina Modocs; not in
a civilized warfare—not in accordance with modern
military tactics, but by the bullet of the high-way robber
and midnight assassin.   Even ex-Sheriff King, although
in his own house, sitting by his own fireside, reading
the news of the day; came unfortunately to the end of
his earthly career through the stealthiness of these sub-
tle villians, who blackened their faces and hands to
disguise their identity and race, and then crept up slyly
and pushed the door open as easily as possible and demanded him to surrender.

Daniel Baker, too, as peaceable and harmless a man
as could be found in the county, was shot in his own
yard, after nightfall, by these inhuman bandits.

It is a misnomer to call the Lowrie war in Robeson
county by any other name than the war of the Bush-
men, or the Bushman War.   It was waged on the part
of Henry Berry Lowrie and brothers in a spirit of revenge.   They wished to retaliate on the white race because the Home Guard of the county found Allen Lowrie, their father; and William Lowrie, their brother, re-
ceivers of stolen goods from various parts of the sur-
rounding country in the month of February, 1864, and
having courtmartialed them and found them guilty,
sentenced them to be shot.   There is but one opinion
in regard to this whole matter among the lawabiding
citizens of Robeson county, and that is that Allen Lowrie, the old man, as he is termed, should have acted a
better part to his white neighbors, who had often be-
friended him, than to have received into his house stolen
goods, taken from his neighbors, and then found to endeavor to screen himself and his son William from

punishment. The verdict of the public is that he was
"particeps criminis," equally guilty with his son William, and that the Home Guard did right in passing
sentence of death on them both and in carrying that
sentence into execution. And right here is a moral
lesson: "The way of the transgressor is hard;" "Vengeance is mine and I will repay, saith the Lord," "The
wicked live out half their days." Behold see! Henry
Berry Lowrie and his associates in crime have gone to
the criminals bourne, "to answer for the deeds done in
the flesh," and may their like never again appear on
this world's arena, for they were the veriest cowards
the most arrant poltroons, that ever disgraced the an-
nals of warfare.

A GEOGRAPHICAL AND TOPOGRAPHICAL
DESCRIPTITION OF SCUFFLETOWN. *

Scuffletown proper is located a little to the north-
west of the centre of Robeson county, the centre being
near Pates about 15 miles north-west of Lumberton, on
the Carolina Central Railway. Eight miles north-westward of Lumberton, on the Carolina Central Railway,
is the station of Moss Neck. Seven miles from Moss
Neck, on the Carolina Central Railway, is the station of
Red Banks, between Moss Neck and Red Banks are
Eureka and Blue's store, so that properly speaking
the Carolina Central Railway cuts into parts the
territory of Scuffletown, which extends on both sides
of the railway tracks some three or four miles, inter-

*Scuffletown, in the common parlance of the country, means a large Indian set-
tlement, without streets or public buildings, having no municipal laws or regula-
tions.

spersed with branches, swamps, and bays. It is a
part of the great swamp district of North Carolina below the sand hills. Standing at Lumberton, the county site, and looking north-westward you see the Ten
Mile Swamp, with Dockery's mill on it (formerly Rhode's
mill), then the Big Raft Swamp, Richland Swamp, Burnt
Sawmp, Bear Swamp, all north of the railway track, tra-
versing the country and running into Lumber River
south of the Carolina Central Railway. North of the
railway track "the Lowrie Band" never committed a
murder. South of the railway track runs Lumber River;
and paralel with Lumber River runs Back Swamp for
twenty miles, the river and swamp being at some places
two miles apart, at others three miles. On Back
Swamp, about ten miles from Inman's bridge across
Lumber River is the place where the Lowrie Robbers
kept their secret camp. Around Moss Neck station are
the scenes of their boldest murders and assassinotions.

This part of Robeson county was doubtless first settled by the ancestors of the present Indians, on account
poverty of the soil and the half inundated condition of
that region, it being within the reach of their means, or
in other words, lands there being cheap. In wet weather,
when much rain has fallen, and the Lumber River and
its tributaries rise, this region is almost flooded, and remains so for some considerable time. In summer a
luxuriant undergrown covers all the swamps and low
places, and even the pine land; while in winter the
streams are full of water and the swamps more ex-
tensive. The growth is sweet gum, black gum, maple,
ash, popular, cypress, post oak, white oak, hickory and
the gallberry bush in abundance. In the margins of the
swamps the yellow jessamine, poison oak and bamboo

vines grow luxuriantly and stretch out eccentrically, making almost an impenetrable abatis; in short, Scuffle-town is a tract of country interspersed and traversed by swamps, covered at wide intervals with hills, with here and there a log cabin out of half dozen of rude and simple construction; sometimes, however, a half dozen of these huts are in sight of each other.

They are great lovers of tobacco, and are always begging a chew of tobacco from those they meet up with. An anecdote is handed down in regard to Duncan Mc-Alpin, a former Sheriff of Robeson. He lived on the borders of Scuffletown, near Philadelphus Presbyterian Church, at the mills on Richland Swamp now owned by W. J. Brown. It is related of Duncan McAlpin that whenever he would meet an Indian on the road, know-ing the habit of begging tobacco, that he would say: "How do you—how do you? Can't you give me a chew of tobacco? Good bye—good bye."

If a traveler wishes to visit a Scuffletown shanty he will be compelled to leave the public road and take a foot-path leading through the woods, across branches and swamps, until he reaches a worn fence made of pine rails, inclosing a half cleared patch of land con-taining three or four acres, in the centre of which gen-erally stands the Indian cabin, constructed of pine poles about five or six inches in diameter, notched one above the other until it reaches the height of eight feet and then covered with pine boards; the chimney built against one end of the house on the outside of poles and clay as far up as the body of the house goes, and the balance of the chimney with sticks and clay, where it narrows to the funnel or smoke hole; a door is cut on the front side and the chinks stopped with clay; no windows generally; sometimes a cut hole is left on the door with numerous peep holes in the body of the cabin. A little distance from the cabin will be found in the yard a well of water, or rather a hole dug in the ground, surrounded with a cypress gum or curb to keep the children from falling in and getting drowned. In the corner of the chimney on the outside will be found a half barrel sawed off and set up on boards one foot above the ground for running off lye, from wood ashes, for the purpose of making soap, the other half of the barrel being used as a washtub. A poor, half-starved fice dog, used for hunting "possums" and "wild varmints," will generally be found inside of the inclosure. The two or three acres cleared are ploughed and planted in corn, potatoes and rice, which come up puny, grow puny and mature puny. The woman of the house commonly has a baby at the breast, and from a half dozen to a dozen children playing outside of the enclosure in the woods. The bed is made on the floor (generally a clay floor); two or three stools to sit on; no division in the cabin, one apartment comprising the whole establishment.

The above picture is true of the great majority of the Indians, but there are a few honorable exceptions. The Oxendines lived in better style and in much more comfortable dwellings; in fact, were well-to-do citizens, whilst the old set of the Lowrie family lived in good, comfortable framed houses, several of them being good mechanics, or house carpenters.

ETHICAL SCIENCE IN SCUFFLETOWN.

The habits of the Indian are peculiar and eccentric,

sometimes assuming a religious aspect as austere as the
most rigid Pharisee could desire, at other times plung-
ing headlong into immoral excesses degrading to human
nature. Pilfering chickens; stealing pigs and killing
sheep for mutton were of frequent occurance among
the denizens of Scuffletown from time immemorial. A
love for spirituous liquors characterized the who population with some few exceptions. The entire race are
intemperate whenever they have the means of gratify-
ing their taste for spirituous liquors, and when under
the influence of liquor they are remarkably quarrel-
some and fussy, often fighting and cutting and stabbing
each other with knives, or shooting each other with
guns or pistols. But notwithstanding these immoral
evils, nearly all Indians, when they arrive at years of
discretion, join either the Baptist or Methodist church
in Scuffletown, which they claim as their church or
churches, being supplied with ministers of the race, educated, licensed and ordained in their peculiar style.

Ever since the Methodist denomination had a circuit
in the county the ministers of that denomination preach-
ed regularly to them, and seemed to outsiders to take an
unusual interest in their spiritual welfare, sometimes admitting to membership, on the profession of their faith,
in the course of the year as many as fifty or sixty. Presbyterian ministers also labored assiduously among them
for a number of years. The Baptist denomination also
sent their ministers in among them to impart spiritual
instruction to their benighted minds.

Since the late war between the States, they have shut
the doors of their churches against all ministers of the
white race and installed in their places in the pulpit persons of their own race.

THE ORIGIN OF SCUFFLETOWN.

When the Scotch first commenced settling in Robeson
county in 1747, after the disasterous battle of Culloden,
(Robeson being then a part of Bladen County) the ancestors of the Locklears, Revels, Cumbos and Chavis' of
today were living where their decendants now live. After the Revolutionary War, the Lowries moved down
into scuffletown and built on the place now known as
the "Harper Ferry place," and kept a ferry there across
Lumber River.   In process of time the Ransoms came
from Halifax county and took up their abode in this settlement.   The Woods' came from Sampson ; the Oxendines from Franklin, also the Cummings', the Goins and
the Braboys.   The Jacobs, Hunts, Morgans, Scotts and
Dials, made their way to Robeson and lived.   James
Murphy lived on the farm now owned by the heirs of
the late Daniel H. McLean, near Maxton on the Carolina Central Railway.   He amassed considerable property and was the owner of slaves.   He married a Cumbo
—a half-breed Tuscarora Indian woman, with a good
countenance.   He left Robeson county about 1792,
with one of the Hunts, and settled on the Great Pee Dee
in South Carolina, near Hunt's Bluff.

The Bell family lived on Saddle Tree Swamp, some
ten or twelve miles from Lumberton on the old stage
road from Lumberton to Fayetteville. One of the family,
namely : Hardy Bell, moved to Lumberton about 1840,
and commenced merchandising.   He succeded in this
line of business very well until he died.   For several
years he was the most prominent merchant in Lumberton, Lumberton being called in Robeson "Hardy Bell's
town," as a burlesque.

They married and intermarried with each other so often that the distinctive features of one was represent- tative of all. Straight black hair, high cheek bones, straight backs and great muscular power characterized the whole race. Traces of the Indian and Anglo-Saxon race can be discovered in the contour of their faces and observed in their demeanor and deportment. As a race they are remarkably superstitious. They believe in fairies, elfs, spirits, ghosts and goblins, and in conjura- tion. They are as a race very prolific. It is no un- common occurrence to find women among them who have born a dozen of children, and some few as many as fifteen or sixteen. They generally, as a race, not- withstanding their love for whiskey, die of old age ; sel- dom sick—seldom in bad health. By the census of 1860 Robeson county contained the extraordinary number of 1,459. Before the late war Scuffletown demoralized the entire slave population and not a few of the "white trash," whilst the interminable diabolism of the Scuffle- tonians forever kept the State Docket in the county crowded with cases, so much so that in each and every year an extra term of court had to be held to finish the cases on the docket, and the worst feature in the whole business was that the county had to "foot the bills," or pay the costs in almost every trial, even to paying jail fees; consequently taxes have ever been high in Robe- son when compared with other counties in the State, so that in the language of the immortal Cicero, we might exclaim, somewhat paraphrased : Quandier, oh! Scuffle- town, abutere nostru patientia?" "(How long, oh! Scuffletown, will you abuse our patience?.")

CONDITION OF AFFAIRS IN ROBESON.

This chapter will give the true condition of affairs in
Robeson county, commencing in the latter part of the
year 1864, and continuing until the latter part of 1870.
At the time the Lowrie robbers commenced their operations in the year 1864, all our able men were at the
front, fighting for rights and homes, while their unprotected families were exposed to a band of merciless
marauders, who, when requisition was made by the
Confederate authorities for their labor on our fortifications, betook themselves to the forests and swamps.

That portion of the county in which this gang organized and commenced operations was confined to Scuffletown, as has been made to appear by false representa-
tions as to the locality. The Lowries lived in Scuffletown. Old Allen Lowrie, held in contempt the common Scuffletonians, purchased a tract of land from a
white man, who was a small farmer, in a neighborhood
which comprised families equal in point of education, refinement and wealth to any community in the county
of Robeson or elsewhere throughout the State. The immediate vicinity in which commenced the horrible
scenes of plunder, so soon to be followed by bloodshed,
was not thickly settled, the plantations being large; consequently families in some instances lived a little remote
from each other. This neighborhood is situated on the
west side of Lumber River, about twelve miles north-
west of Lumberton, and fifteen south from Floral College.

At the time of their organization in the year 1864
there were no men at home, except a few who were ex-
empt from service by age and other causes; in some

families there was no gentleman left. The citizens of
upper Robeson, becoming aware of our utter helpless-
ness to defend ourselves, formed into a Home Guard
and very kindly came down to endeavor to learn who
comprised the gang, their strength, and also to become
conversant with their mode and line of operation.
They quartered themselves at McLaughlin's Bridge,
on Lumber River, for about two weeks. Within that
time they were convinced that their force was entirely
too weak to effect much with the gang, and it was
positively learned that it numbered as high as forty or
fifty. An appeal for aid was sent to Richmond county
The Home Guard of that county, though few in number,
hesitated not to join the gallant few who were chaffing
to be in action. They soon succeeded in capturing
and killing their leader, William Lowrie, and his father,
Allen Lowrie, as his house was their headquarters, and
therein was found some of the stolen property. This
did little towards ending the troubles in Robeson; it
ceased only for a short time, to break out with renewed
zeal and ardor. Younger sons, with those allied by
blood, re-organized, and with the Indian stealthiness
and spirit of revenge, go forth plundering and spreading terror throughout the community by their un-
limited acts of lawlessness and terrible threats of
vengeance. In the meantime peace being declared, our
men returned, worn down and disheartened, not only
by the turn affairs had taken, but also the condition in
which they found their families. For months the robber
gang go on undisturbed—and why? Simply this: those
who were willing and ready to make an attempt to arrest them, could get no aid from others in their vicinity.
When they would go and request them to "come with

us and we will stop it," almost the invarible reply was,
"No, if they will let us alone, we will let them alone,"
refusing even to lend their guns to those without arms.
Some gave as a reason that they lived too near the line
of their operations; their hands were tied, for if the
robbers found it out they would be revenged on their
persons or property. A refusal in such cases seemed
to say: They may kill my friend, or devastate my
neighbor's property, but if they will let me and my interests alone, why then I will be content for them to remain forever at large."

Prompted by selfish motives to refuse to aid and abet
the noble men who would have risked life and all to
secure peace and quiet for those in more immediate vicinity of the gang, they thereby secured to themselves,
by permitting those living fiends to go unmolested, a
punishment equal in some degree to those who did all
in their power to arrest them. Nearly every family for
miles, who was possessed of any property, were annoyed
by their visits and depredations.

The first election held there after the surrender, as in
almost every other county in the State, placed radicals
in office; and in our county some of her petty officers
assumed more power in the control of local affairs than
the Constitution of the State allowed; yet they were
quietly permitted to use that authority. Such was our
condition when the citizens of Robeson rose up to
throw off the yoke that was galling them sorely. They
started out, determined not only to demolish the robber
gang, but all against whom they had unquestionable evidence as being friends and informants for the gang.
They killed one or two of their allies; the supposed per-

petrators were pointed out by friends of the robber
gang, and evidence taken sufficiently to outlaw, by a
Radical Judge, a company of nine as noble young men,
from good families, as our country can boast, and forced
them to flee beyond the limits of their native State to seek
that protection they could not claim within her borders.
To further intimidate the citizens of Robeson the hue and
cry of "Ku Klux, Ku Klux," is raised, and loud threats
by her officials of Kirk and his men are heard. Some of
our best men were arrested and kept before a "Justice"
Court for days. All the young men who were engaged
in hunting the robbers stood in daily expectation of
undergoing the same ordeal. Surrounded on the one
hand by the robber gang and their friends, through the
thick pine woods, and, to a white man, the almost
impenetrable swamps; on the other, Radical officials
dispensing their so-called justice to the noble fellows
who would have captured them, and you have the
situation. Instances could be given where young men
received orders from the High Sheriff to search the
houses of some of the suspected parties, and on obeying their orders were notified to appear before the
"Justice of the Peace" in Lumberton, to answer charges preferred against them for ill treatment to inmates
of said houses. On appearing for trial, the parties al-
leged to have been ill treated, swore in open court to
the falsity of the charge. They were therefore neces-
sitated to release the men without having a chance to
vent their individual spite on the heads of their innocent prisoners. Thus the citizens of Robeson were in-
timidated. Their situation not being realized beyond
their county limits, they were branded in many places
throughout the county as cowards; but could their

nightly vigils and midnight tramps, with knapsack and
gun, all be chronicled; their days of exposure to cold,
and often to hunger, in the dense woods watching for
the enemy, be recorded. "Cowards of Robeson" would
be changed to her gallant heroes.

STATEMENT OF REV. C. M. PEPPER.

This chapter comprises the statement of Rev. C. M.
Pepper, of the North Carolina Conference, giving a correct account of the state of affairs during his sojourn in
Robeson county.   He says: I resided in the neighborhood in which the Lowries lived in the year 1865.   I
was well acquainted with Allen Lowrie, the father of
Henry Berry, and have, I suppose, often seen the latter,
as I knew several of the old man's sons, though not
well enough to distinguish all of them by name.

Allen Lowrie was a sort of chief in the community
in which he lived.   He attended church every Sabbath.
He was perhaps the wealthiest, and most intelligent and
respectable of all the free people in that community.
He was a tall, fine looking Indian, with straight hair, and
a physiognomy that indicated Indian blood greatly
predominant in his extraction.   He lived in a comfortable frame building, had a farm, and made a good
living.   He was respected by the whites of the community and looked up to by the colored.

I do not know so much about his sons, but if I re-
member correctly they were all of them like their
father in complexion, and hair indicating a large mixture
of Indian blood.

I found when I reached the neighborhood of that

settlement that this race had been in some excitement,
the cause of which was an attempt on the part of the
authorities to put them in the army. Some of them
were skulking in the bushes and swamps, and among
these were some of the sons of Lowrie. I was startled
at the account they gave me of the murder of a good
man, an excellent citizen (J. P. Barnes) of that community, whom I had known for years. This was about
the first of the long list of outrages which have been
perpetrated in that community since that time; this was
the beginning, I may say, of a reign of terror.

Soon after the murder of James Barnes the people
were almost petrified with fear at the intelligence of
the fact that there was an organized band of marauders, of how great a number no one knew. We had
been informed, or did afterwards learn, that this band
was composed of Yankee prisoners, escaped from the
Florence prison in South Carolina, of Indians, and, as
we supposed, of some few mean white men and slaves.

The community was terror-stricken as they heard of
new depredations and outrages committed each night;
almost every day we heard that the robbers had entered
a house the night before, ransacked and taken whatever they wanted, caroused, insulted or attacked some
of the family, and producing terror and consternation.
In every instance they took all the ammunition and
liquor they could find, and generally seized or broke
the fire-arms. There was a panic in the community;
so great was the fear that persons were afraid to step
out into the yard after dark—everything was done before night. The doors were bolted securely; the inmates would gather around the fire and sit with hearts
palpitating at every sound they heard, momentarily ex-

pecting the appearance of the dreaded band of desperadoes. No one knew how many were in the gang,
or who belonged to it, except a few who had been recognized. They went in the dark, and on entering a
house extinguished the lights, or only those entered
who were strangers to the household. The gang had
been estimated as high as fifty in number, and we were
satisfied that the Lowries had in it a prominent place.
The evidence was satisfactory that one of them killed
Mr. Barnes, and some of them had been identified
amongst the clan.

I was boarding at that time at Mrs. Nash's, widow of
Dr. Nash, who was a son of Judge Nash. Her house
was right on the border of Lumber River. It was on
an island in that river, as we afterwards learned, and in
a quarter of a mile of Mrs. Nash's, that the robbers
rendezvoused during the day, and from this den sallied
forth at night. They visited Mrs. Nash's house on
several occasions, but did her no damage in any way.
We had prepared for them, or at least made out our
plan of receiving them. I advised Mrs. Nash if they
should come to treat them with as much kindness as
possible. They came the first time when I was from
home, and although there was not a white man on the
premises, and the three ladies were almost paralyzed
with fear, Mrs. Nash went out and spoke to them in the
yard. The first intimation the ladies had of their
presence was from the servant girl, who came in
hurriedly and told them that the robbers were there,
and had sent her to tell the ladies to send out all the
keys at once. Mrs. McCormick, a sister of Mrs. Nash,
handed the key basket to the girl, and told her to tell
them, if they pleased, not to enter the house, that they

were alone.   Mrs. Nash was more calm; she stopped
the girl and bade her light a candle, that she would go
with her.   The other ladies objected strongly to this;
but she thought best to put on as bold a front as possible,
which she did, and stepped out to speak with them.   She
addressed them in a pleasant tone, and told them that
they were three unprotected ladies, requested and
begged them not to harm their persons, that they could
have anything they wanted.   The man who seemed to
be leader, and who was an escaped Yankee prisoner,
was completely disarmed and tamed by the eloquence
of her tongue and blandness of her manners.   In the
case of their leader, "the lion seemed changed into the
lamb," and he said. "Madam, we are obliged to have
something to eat."   "Certainly," said Mrs. Nash, "walk
into the house and be seated, and I will have supper
prepared."   Two strange white men came in, filthy and
ragged, well armed with double-barreled shot guns, &c.

They sat down, and while supper was being prepared Mrs. Nash entered into conversation with them,
and entertained them as few ladies in North Carolina
could have done under the circumstances.   She told
them of the gang of robbers in the neighborhood, endeavored, and no doubt succeeded, in making the
impression, on their mind that she did not even suspect
them of being connected with the gang, and begged
their protection against their assault.   While she was
talking with these men, quite a number of their accomplices were stationed as a guard outside, and standing in the yard awaiting orders.   After a while they
seemed to get impatient for booty, and began to complain,
and several times one of the men walked out and
cursed them.   After supper they remained until a late

hour; sang some for the ladies, and had Mrs. Nash to
perform some pieces for them on the piano. They
finally bade the ladies good night and went off,
taking nothing except a case knife, to which the fingers
of one of the company stuck, and which was afterwards returned.

In a few nights they came again, dressed in broad-
cloth and boots, shaved and washed, making really a
genteel appearance. I was again from home, or rather
I was off on duty. They remained as before until a
late hour of the night, and left, doing no damage.

The third time they came I was at home. Hearing
their heavy footfalls on the long piazza of the old man-
sion, the ladies insisted that Mr. D. M. McCormick
(who was there also) and I should retire to another
room, which I afterwards concluded Mr. McCormick
was very willing to do. I wished to see them, but
yielded to the entreaties of the ladies, and we walked
out of the room just in time to avoid their knowledge
of our presence. This time they were evidently very
uneasy. The Home Guard, in considerable force, was
stationed four miles up the river, and in search of the
robbers. They seemed very restless, sat with their
guns across their knees, and were not so pleasant and
communicative as before. Presently they arose hurriedly, stepped out at the door, and were gone for a few
minutes, when the silence was broken by several loud
reports from shot guns, then all was quiet and still as
death for half an hour. They then walked into the
house again.

In our room we had two double-barreled shot guns,
one six-shooter and one rifle. I proposed to Mr. Mc-

Cormick that we should take them, but he seemed rather nervous for the undertaking, and I then made the proposition to slip out at the window and go to where we knew the Home Guard were stationed. This seemed to him also to be rather perilous, so we let them slide. This time they did not stay long, and when they left, left not to return again. On the next morning, to our surprise, we were informed by the negroes that they had left one of their number in the negro cabin sick, and requested Mrs. Nash, through the servants, to let him stay there until he would get well. Mrs. Nash went out to see and speak with him. He told her that he had been with the robber gang only for concealment and sustenance; that he had never joined with them in their marauding operations, as he was taken sick the first night he reached Allen Lowrie's, and had been sick up to that time. He also told her that he was one of the escaped Yankee prisoners from Florence, and was with the band because he had nowhere else to go. He gave his name as Owen T. Wright. He had with him a Bible, which had the appearance of having been much used. His plausible story was received by Mrs. Nash, who began at once to sympathize with him. She had the negroes to wash and dress him in clean clothes, carry him into her dwelling house and put him in a comfortable bed. This was scarcely done before the house was surrounded by a company of armed men, who proved to be the Home Guard. I walked out and spoke to one of them in the yard. He asked me hurriedly about the Yankee. I stated to him the facts of the case, and others coming up and hearing my statement, rushed to the room where the invalid Yankee was, and I suppose would, but for the interposition of the kind

lady, have put an end to his life without taking him out
of sight of the house. Pocahontas-like, Mrs. Nash plead
for his life and stood between him and destruction until
the excitement had subsided. They consented to take
him and give the case an investigation. Putting him
in a cart, they hurried him off towards their headquarters; from there he was sent to Lumberton and a
comfortable room provided for him by Mrs. S. A. Mc-
Queen, where he remained for a few days. Sherman's
men made a raid into Lumberton, and carried him off
with the rest of their booty.

The evening previous to their visit to Mrs. Nash's
they went to the house of Allen Lowrie, where they
found William Lowrie, his son, who was identified as
one of the gang, mending or fixing his gun. They arrested him. They searched his father's house, and
finding much of the stolen property concealed in his
house, arrested him also. A brief court-martial was
held. Allen and William Lowrie were both found
guilty and sentenced to be shot. William attempted to
make his escape, but a shot from one of the company
brought him down, but did not kill him. They carried
him to Mr. Robert McKinzie's, where they had several
others, who had been also arrested and held in confinement by members of the same company for examination. Sufficient evidence was not obtained to crimi-
nate any of the party except Allen and William Lowrie;
the others were released. According to the rules of
war a certain number or men were detailed to execute
the sentence. Allen requested time to pray, which
was granted him. They were then led out and bound
—a short pause—a loud report—and the prisoners fell
lifeless to the earth. This trial and execution meted

out summary justice to one of the notorious gang and an
accomplice in crime. who, though not yet recognized
among the desperadoes, was as guilty as those who
perpetrated the crimes.

The event of Lowries' death which I have just mentioned, it is thought, kindled afresh in the bosom of
Henry Berry the fires of revenge, which are always so
difficult to extinguish in the breasts of Indians. Nothing would quench that fire but blood.

But now for a time the robberies in the community
ceased and for a while the minds of the people were com-
paratively quiet. The assault upon them by the Home
Guard seemed to scatter the band and destroy their organization. Before that they had entered nearly every
house in an area of six or ten miles square, the particulars of which, and the names of those robbed, will be giv-
en by one better acquainted with the facts than I am.

Henry Berry went to his home, and after a little
time he became so bold that he did not pretend to conceal himself at all. The other negroes went home also.
The people felt for several months that there was an
end to trouble of this sort; and doubtless there would
have been but few more outrages committed after that
but for the remarkable turn which government matters
took at the close of the war. Emboldened by the poli-
cy of the dominant party, they commenced the work of
revenge, in which they were so anxious to engage, such
as robbing and murdering those in opposition to them.

We will now proceed to give a list of the crimes as
they were perpetrated, and every outrage committed
by the Lowrie band, as it occurred:

J. P. BARNES.

The first murder committed by the Lowries was that
of James P. Barnes, a most estimable man and good
citizen.   He was shot about 9 o'clock a. m., December
21st, A. D., 1864, and died in the afternoon of the same
day.   The particulars of his murder are these: He was
post-master at Clay Valley, in Robeson county, about a
mile and a half from his residence, and was on his way
to the post office, when he was fired on by three men
in ambush, twenty-eight shot lodging in his breast.   He
had fallen when Henry B. Lowrie ran up with his gun
cocked; Mr. Barnes recognized him, and entreated him
not to shoot him any more, that he would die from the
wounds already received, but regardless of his look of
agony, or his earnest pleading, he raised his gun and
discharged it in the face of Mr. Barnes, knocking out
several teeth, and taking off part of his under-jaw.
The cruel, heartless wretches then left him alone in the
backwoods, almost in the last agonies of death.   The
hour passed for him to be at the office, but still he did
not come.   His brother, Dr. John A. Barnes, who was
there, knowing his strict punctuality to business, and
his rigid observance of every duty, felt somewhat alarm-
ed at his prolonged absence, and started to his house to
learn the cause.   About three-fourths of a mile from
the office he found him, wounded in the manner above
stated. He removed him as quickly as possible, but all
efforts to prolong his life proved unavailing; he died in

NOTE   The view on page 43 illustrates the mill dam near Moss
Neck where Mr. J. P. Barnes was murdered.   The man standing
near a clump of trees is where the men were concealed when Mr.
Barnes was passing on his way to his place of business.

a few hours.   Although so badly wounded, the power
of speech was not denied him; he told them it was
Henry Berry Lowrie and two white men whom he did
not recognize; those were supposed to be Yankee
prisoners, who afterwards became members of the band.
Mr. Barnes lived on the Back Swamp, and was a man
very fond of hunting deer and turkeys; he had no
family, and his leisure hours were spent in this way.
Henry Berry Lowrie lived out back of Mr. Barnes, and
was lurking at that time in the woods to avoid being
carried to the forts below Wilmington to work.   It was
then he was making up his band to rob and plunder the
citizens of that community.   Knowing the habits of
Mr. Barnes, and for fear of detection by him, it is supposed for this reason only, he determined to put him out
of the way by murdering him in the cruel manner already described.   There had been some little disagree-
ment between Mr. Barnes, and old man Lowrie about
some cattle, and also some hogs that had been stolen
from Mr. Barnes, but admitting it to be either one or the
other, it was a trivial cause for which to waylay and
murder in cold blood a good man, beloved by all, just
and honest in all his dealings.

J. BRANTLY HARRISS.

The next on record comes the murder of Mr. Harriss.
This occurred in January, 1865.   During the war a
call was made upon the Indian people to work on the
defences below Wilmington.   George Lowrie, a brother of Allen Lowrie, had several sons—two of whom
were carried off, and did work where they were sent.

After remaining there some time, they got furloughs to come home for a few days; they were at home but a short time when Harriss had them arrested as deserters. It seems that prior to this there had been some feud existing between the Lowries and Harriss. However, Harriss had them, and left with them, for the purpose as he stated, of putting them aboard the train at Moss Neck Depot to send them back to their work on the fortifications. On the way thither, when some evil demon took possession of him, he murdered them both, cruelly and inhumanly. A jury of inquest was held over them, and the facts of the murder was clearly set forth on Harriss. A warrant was issued for Harriss' arrest and placed in the hands of Sheriff King on Friday. The Sunday following Harriss was riding out with a woman in his buggy; after she got out of the buggy he went but a short distance when he was shot and killed. The young Lowries killed by Harriss were near relatives of H. B. Lowrie, and it was H. B. Lowrie that shot Harriss. Harriss was the only man killed by the Lowrie Gang that did not sustain a fair character. He had been living for several years in or near Scuffletown, and was a man feared by all who knew him. He had a wife and two children, but they did not seem to possess much influence over him for good.

ROBBERIES.

It was in February, 1865, that they commenced so openly to rob and plunder. There were a few families that escaped, although each night they were expected by all whom they had not visited. It was certainly a

time to be remembered by all, both old and young.
The nights of mise-able terror and days of dread suspense, which all endured during their operations in the
neighborhood are indescribable. The first place that
the robbers entered a house openly for plunder was
Mrs. Alexander Bullard's.   She was alone in the house
with her five children, her husband being in the army,
when four men, armed and disguised, walked in.   They
told her they wanted her husband's gun and clothing,
which they took without much ceremony. A negro boy,
belonging to Mr. J. D. Bridgers, had a wife at Mrs.
Bullard's; he was in the kitchen, and hearing voices in the
house, with that curiosity characteristic of the race,
slipped out to see who it was.   As soon as he saw the
situation of Mrs. Bullard he turned and ran a mile and
a quarter to his master's, and on reaching the gate, had
only strength to call the name of his young master, and
fainted.   As soon as he could be restored to conscious-
ness, in broken sentences he explained the situation of
Mrs. B. Mr. Bridgers and his son, A. C. Bridgers, (then
15 years of age) armed themselves and the negro boy,
and went as quickly as possible to her aid.   On reaching there they found all quiet; the robbers had gone,
taking the gun and a few articles of wearing apparel.
At this place they behaved quietly, used no insulting
language, nor did not seem to have any desire to frighten
her.

JOHN McNAIR.

Mr. McNair lived in a few miles of the Lowries.   He
carried on a large farm, having many hands in his employ; this necessarily compelled him to have much

building done on his plantation. Several of the Lowries being carpenters, good workmen, and in good
standing among the whites, were employed by Mr.
McNair for this purpose. Being so employed from time
to time, they had the advantage of learning the situation
of affairs in general about the premises, which they
made free use of, much to Mr. McNair's discomfiture.
It may be well to speak here of Mr. McNair's kindness
to many of them, their treatment afterwards showing
how utterly devoid of gratitude they were when it con-
flicted with their love of gain. Mr. McNair was an
excellent farmer, and made much produce for sale.
The Indians having very small farms, many of them
none at all, were often reduced to the necessity of going among the whites to purchase the necessaries of
life. Mr. McNair generously supplied their wants when
they called upon him, never turning them from his
door empty; sometimes they paid him, but as often
failed in making any return for it. The following lines
will show how much he suffered by them pecuniarily,
despite all his kindness to them. Their first visit to his
house for plundei was in April, A. D. 1864. This was
before any regular band of robbers existed, and the
Lowries were not suspected at all as having anything
to do with the stealing at this time that was going on,
but it was afterwards proven to be them by the missing
articles being found in their possession and identified.
At the time of the above mentioned visit they entered
the study, which was apart from the main dwelling, but
in the same enclosure, and took a feather-bed. In the
following June they again entered the study, but as
everything had been removed except one bed-quilt,
they did not get anything but that, and it was found

sometime afterwards in a fodder stack near Allen Lowrie's house. It was supposed that numbers of the gang
had been sleeping in the stack, and as they were operating on a small scale, being about the commencement of
their operations, they were afraid to have anything in
their houses that could be identified in case search was
made. Up to this, and for sometime afterwards, the
citizens of the community did not suspicion the Lowries, and were astonished when some of them were
recognized among the band, as they had heretofore been
considered honest, hard-working people. Old Allen Lowrie, in his youthful days, had been guilty of taking a
sheep which he supposed belonged to an uncle of his,
but it turned out to be the property of a white man.
He was punished for this, and the circumstance almost
entirely forgotten except by some of our oldest citizens,
when the fact of his aiding the robber clan was dis-
closed. In December, 1864, Mr. McNair's gin-house
was burned down, containing twelve or fourteen bales
of cotton and a good many other articles of much value.
In January, 1865, they robbed his smoke-house and
store-room; this time taking a large quantity of pork
and a good many other valuable things. After this,
except an occasional visit to their poultry yard, they
were undisturbed until June, 1867, when they again
entered the study and dining-room. From the study
they took another bed, bolster, pillows, blankets, sheets,
combs, brushes, a quantity of clothing, &c. From the
dining-room they took crockery-ware, knives, silver
forks and spoons. On the night of the 23rd of January,
1868, they entered the dwelling-house by means unknown to the family, though the probability is that some
of the gang were secreted in the house before the doors

were closed for the night, and after the family were
locked in slumber, admitted the balance of their party.
They entered the bed-room where the family were
sleeping, took the candle from the mantle-piece where
Mrs. McNair had placed it on retiring, lit it with a match,
and searched the entire house thoroughly. They took
from Mr. McNair's pockets his pocket-book containing
one hundred and twenty-five dollars ($125) in money,
valuable notes and other articles. They took his guns,
nearly all the keys in the house, and a fine gold watch.
Four years afterwards, when those brave men killed
Tom Lowrie, they took a watch off his person which
was identified as Mr. McNair's, and returned it to him.
But to return: They robbed the dining-room and pantry,
and searched the pocket of Mrs. McNair's dress, taking
two bunches of keys from it. They then went into a
back room, broke open a trunk, took everything out of
it, evidently searching for money; but finding nothing
but Mrs. McNair's summer clothing, left it piled on the
floor, with the contents of the pocket-book, except the
money, lying on top. About midnight Mr. McNair was
taken with a violent headache, to which he was subject,
and aroused Mrs. McNair to give him something to relieve it. She arose and went to get the candle where
she was sure she had placed it, and it was gone; she un-
locked a closet in her room, and got another candle and
lighted it. She looked around and found Mr. McNair's
clothes missing. On further examination she discovered
that the house had been robbed of a good deal. They
both went out into the yard and about the out-houses,
hoping that the robbers might have dropped some of the
keys; but in this they were disappointed. Between that
and the summer of 1871 they made frequent raids on

the dining-room, pantry and fowl house, each time taking a good supply. At one of their visits about this time, they shot the yard dog on the porch. In all their raids at his house, Mr. McNair did not discover them but once; he found they were in his pantry. They soon learned that they were discovered and made good their retreat. Mr. McNair fired two or three times after them, but they did not return the fire.

In February, 1871, Mr. McNair was on his way to Red Banks; when about a mile or so from the Banks, he met four of the robber clan in a turpentine wagon; they ordered him to stop or they would shoot him. He checked his horse, and Steve Lowrie walked up and caught his bridle; H. B. Lowrie and Boss Strong then went up to him, took him by his hands, one on each side, and inquired if he had a pistol; he told them he had not, and pushed Boss Strong from him. Boss Strong then took his buggy whip and struck him across the head with it one time, and one of the others struck him with his gun; Steve Lowrie then called out and said: "Boys, I told you not to hurt him." Henry Berry then searched his pockets, taking his pocket-book and several letters that he was carrying to the office to be mailed. He handed the letters to Tom Lowrie, and he kept the pocket-book, stepping to one side to examine its contents. After he had satisfied himself as to what it contained, he turned to Mr. McNair and asked him which he preferred, to have his pocket-book and go back home, or for him (H. B. Lowrie) to keep the pocket book and allow Mr. McNair to go on to the Banks. He replied that he had business at the Banks, and he intended going unless they killed him, and he wanted both the pocket-book and letters, which Tom Lowrie had still in possession. Henry Berry gave him the pocket-book, telling him as he had but fifteen dollars ($15) in it he would not take it. Tom Lowrie handed him two of the letters, retaining five. They then told him he could go on, but to say nothing to any one about meeting them; but he paid no attention to the last order. There was a young lady with Mr. McNair at the time, and she was badly frightened.

The last raid made on Mr. McNair was in June, 1871. They entered the dining-room and pantry, this time taking nearly everything they could find, leaving no place unsearched. They took a barrel and a half of flour, a lot of silverware, some clothing, and numerous other articles.

On the morning of the 14th of July, 1871, about daylight, five armed men were seen approaching the house of Mr. McNair. They supposed them to be the militia, who were out at the time in search of the gang. They came up in front of the house, and called Mr. McNair out to them. They conversed with him for perhaps a half hour. Mrs. McNair, thinking that it was some of our men who were tired and hungry, went out and ordered breakfast prepared for them. She knew no better until breakfast was ready, and Mr. McNair came in and told her it was the Lowrie band, and they wanted something to eat. She sent them word to go around to the dining-room, where they would find breakfast waiting. They went into breakfast, taking their arms with them. Their object on this visit was to get Mr. McNair to write a letter for them, to take it down to Lumberton and deliver it to Col. Sinclair and Sheriff McMillan, ordering the release of their wives, who had been arrested a few days previous. Soon after the

robber clan ate their breakfast they left.   Mr. McNair
made ready and went to Lumberton, not only to deliver
the letter to the parties named, but also to use his influence in behalf of the women kept in confinement, for
the people in the country were entirely at their mercy,
and they had made such threats with regard to the
ladies of the community that the excitement was so
great that several families moved from their homes to
places more remote from their lines of action.   Further
particulars with regard to the success of Mr. McNair's
visit to Lumberton will be given more fully hereafter.
A guard of fifty men were proffered Mr. McNair on his
leaving the village, to accompany him home; this he refused, well knowing should he return so accompanied
that it would raise the ire of the robber gang, and as
soon as his guard would leave him he would be liable
to be murdered by them.

Mrs. McNair was left entirely alone (except the servants) during the day of this visit, and suffered much
uneasiness.   She expected they would lurk around the
premises and in the absence of Mr. McNair, return and
commit more of their depredations, but they did not.
She talked to them freely of their frequent robberies
there, which they did not deny.   Her greatest anxiety,
though, was for Mr. McNair's safety.   She feared that
he might be unsuccessful, and they would probably
meet him somewhere on the road on his return, and on
learning the truth would become so enraged as to wreak
their vengeance on him.   They did meet him, but forbore
to injure him personally.   This was on Friday, and
they said if their wives were not released by the following Monday afternoon, that Robeson county would
be deluged in blood; after that time they would know

no man, but would shoot down every one that passed
them; that hitherto they had not interfered with the
women, that they had scorned it, but after then they
might take care, that they were safe no longer. Many
such threats were made by them on this occasion,
which is needless to mention.

A half-mile below Mr. McNair's, on the Lumberton
road, they called in at Mr. McRaken's and ordered his
wife to cook some provisions for them, which they had
with them.   They stayed until it was cooked, behaving
very quietly.   They took it and left; came on a short
distance to Mr. Patterson's, and finding no one at the
house but the ladies, they remained only a short time,
but proceeded to a field where Mr. McN. Patterson
(who afterwards assisted in the killing of Steve Lowrie)
and his father were at work.   They called Mr. Mc P. to
them and conversed with him for some time, making
threats to him also as to what they intended doing with
the ladies of the community. They then came on to the
house of Mr. Jas. D. Bridgers, where they remained
until nearly time for McNair's return, when they left,
going down the road in the direction which Mr. Mc-
Nair would come.   A further account of this will be
given in the chapter containing the particulars of their
depredations at Mr. Bridgers'.   The United States soldiers, as well as the militia in command of Capt. F. M.
Wishart, were stationed only a few miles above.   The
friends of the robber gang, scattered here and there
throughout the county, would convey to them the
whereabouts of the enemy, and thus they succeeded in
eluding them on every occasion.

RICHARD TOWNSEND.

On the night or the 14th of December, 1864, they
went to the house of Mr. Richard Townsend and took
his gun. It was sometime after supper; Mrs. T. was
sitting in her room, with all the doors of the house
open. She heard some one speak to a servant in an
adjoining room, and immediately afterwards footsteps
approaching towards her room door; she raised her
eyes, and standing at the door was a man she had
never seen before. He asked her where her husband
was; she pointed to the bed, where Mr. T. was asleep;
he then asked why he was not in the army, and went
on to say that he (the robber) was hunting deserters,
and was out of ammunition, and wanted Mr. Townsend to give him some powder and his gun. She told
him that he was not hunting deserters; that he was one
himself, with a courage and fearlessness that belong
only to the ladies of the South. "Well," replied the
robber, "If I am, what is that to you? Give me a shirt,
the gun and powder." Mrs. T. then arose from her
seat, awoke her husband, who went to get the gun,
while she got the shirt. The things brought, the bandit took them, bidding them both good evening, joined
his party, who were awaiting him on the piazza at the
front of the house, and departed for that night. They
were there several times afterwards, the particulars of
which will be seen on another page.

JACKSON TOWNSEND.

In a few weeks after their visit to Mr. Richard Townsend's they called at the house of his brother Jackson.

He was in the army, and no one with his wife, except
her children and the servants. Mrs. T. had just gone
in from supper, and hearing footsteps on the piazza,
looked out through the window, and discovered a man
standing in the piazza, near the window; he was a
white man. As soon as he saw he was discovered he raised
the window, and Mrs. T. pulled it down; he then put
his gun under it and raised it again. This time she
stepped to one side, and he came in. He asked her why
she did not open the door. She replied that she did not
know there was any one there. He was the only one
that came in on this occasion, and he would not suffer
the doors to be opened. Mrs. Townsend looked out to
see if there were any more, and counted five others on
the piazza. The one in the house asked her if she saw
them all. She told she did. He said: "No, you haven't;
I have a dozen more out in the road." He then searched
the house, taking the gun and several other articles.
He then left. A few nights afterwards they came again.
This time two entered the house—one a very tall, heavy-
built man, answering the description of one William-
son, from Columbus county, who was afterwards
identified as belonging to the robber clan, and killed by
some unknown person or persons near his old home in
Columbus. His companion was a very small man, also
white. The tall man did all the searching that was
done each time. They asked Mrs. Townsend for wine;
she told them she had some she was keeping for sickness. They told her to get it. She brought it out, in
a demijohn and jug. They took it all and set it in the
piazza; but when they started off they gave her back
the demijohn, telling her she might keep that and they

would take the other, as she would not need it all for
sickness. They called a few nights afterwards for the
demijohn, all took a drink, and gave her back the
balance. The tall man was in the dining room, and
she requested his comrade to ask him to come out,
which he did. As he came out she saw that he was
wrapped in one of her blankets. She told him it was
hers, but he said no, he had brought it with him. She
believed it to be false, and was convinced of the fact
when she found hers was missing. Mrs. Townsend
went through some of the rooms with him, all the time
watching, as she thought, his every move, but he was
such an adept at stealing that he carried off a good
many articles that she did not see him take. After they
were through plundering, they told her they wanted
her horse and buggy, and on her objecting, told her
they would take them whether she was willing or not.
They took a lighted candle, went out to examine the
buggy, and finding it insufficient for their purpose,
left without taking it. They proceeded again to Mr.
Richard Townsend's, one mile distant, and took his
buggy, carriage and horses, and went on to Mr. Joseph
Thompson's and Henry Bullock Jr's. They took a
negro to drive the carriage, and sent them back just
before daylight the next morning, very much jaded.
Sometime during the year 1865 they visited Mr. Townsend's again. This time they beat and banged against
the doors, and on failing to get in, retired a short distance and fired two guns into the house, but did no
further damage. They robbed his smoke-house after
this, taking a large lot of bacon. In April, 1869, Mrs.
Townsend, with her sister, went into a back room, and
discovered a dark man under the bed. She retired

hastily to inform her husband; but he, guessing from her hasty retreat that he had been seen, sprung through the window and made his escape. The rest of the gang were waiting for the family to retire, and this fellow, who had by some means gotten into the house, was to admit the others. The tracks of their party were plainly discernible the next morning in the garden, where they had stolen all of Mrs. Townsend's onions. They came several times afterwards, but did no damage, except to kill their yard dog. Their purposes were so often thwarted there that they desisted any further molestation at his house.

JOSEPH THOMPSON.

The first visit to Mr. Thompson's by the clan was in March, 1865. Only white men entered the house, eight in number. It was after night, and they came up cheering and shouting, "the Yankees are coming." The first thing they did after entering the house was to take Mr. Thompson, with three other gentlemen who were his guests for the night, prisoners. They behaved here very roughly, cursing loudly and firing off their guns in the house. Mrs. Thompson, an aged lady, insisted on their giving her some articles that they were taking, which she prized, but they refused, at the same time firing a pistol over her head, the contents lodging in the wall beyond From their conduct on this occasion they were undoubtedly drunk, as it was a short time previous to this that they had stolen a large quantity of brandy from Mr. Bullock. They took guns, clothing and bed-clothing to a large amount. They took the hats of the gentlemen who were there, and left them to go home bareheaded. They went so far as to parole the men as prisoners of war. The Lowries remained in the yard receiving and stowing away the stolen property.

In the year 1870 they visited Mr. T. again, this time, as they avowed, for the purpose of murdering a man by the name of Perry, who was superintending Mr. Thompson's farm. When the militia were ordered out in the county, Perry was among them. He, with a small squad of men, fired on the robber gang. Some of their friends and informants reported to them that Perry was at the head of the party. This was sufficient to arouse their resentment, and it was their intention on this occasion to sate their thirst for revenge by taking his life. They had been prowling around Mr. Thompson's plantation for some time for this purpose, but Mr. Perry being very cautious, they had not succeeded in meeting him. On this night Mr. T. was walking out, when he was hailed and arrested by three armed men, headed by Stephen Lowrie. He demanded of Mr. T. the whereabouts of Mr. Perry, and compelled him to conduct them to his house, saying they intended killing him that night. Mr. Perry, hearing voices and suspecting it to be the robber clan, made his escape through a back door, thus eluding them. After they learned that Mr. Perry had escaped, they returned with Mr. Thompson to his house, and asked him for some tobacco and bacon, which he gave them, well knowing that they would take it if he refused.

HENRY BULLOCK, JR.

In February, 1865, the robber clan drove up to Mr. Henry Bullock's in the vehicles pressed into their ser-

vice at Mr. Richard Townsend's. On reaching his
gate, they sprang out, entered his yard and burst into
his house. Eight men came in, several others remaining in the yard; one of those in the house kept his hat
pulled over his face, fearing, no doubt, that he might be
recognized. The captain of the band sat down in a
corner by the hearth, and ordered Mr. Bullock in a
very peremptory manner to "raise a light, or they
would do it for him." With that cool courage that the
nature of the case demanded he replied, "If you can
make a light quicker than I can, you may do it," but
the renegade Yankee kept his seat, allowing Mr. B. to
make the fire. After he was through he looked around
on his unwelcome visitors, and discovered seven ransacking his house from garret to cellar. Their leader
kept his seat quietly during the plundering, no doubt
having issued all orders necessary before reaching their
destination. Those in the house threw the things from
the windows, when they were taken by their comrades
on the outside and stowed away in the waiting vehicles. The Lowries had just commenced their career
of stealing and plundering, and had not grown bold
enough to enter houses when there was the least
probability of their being recognized. They carried
off a large quantity of clothing, bed-clothing, &c. Mr.
Bullock had a lot of brandy on hand, of his own make,
of which they partook pretty freely while there, and
carried off about thirty gallons. After they were
through plundering, they turned to Mr. Bullock and
told him they would not hurt him; he replied: "The
d—l you won't." They referred to his person, but
he considered himself badly treated in a pecuniary
point of view. They visited Mr. B. again after this;

there were only three this time, supposed to be a portion of the band, or at least co-operating with the Lowries.   It was afterwards learned that they were deserters from the Confederate ranks, two of whom were
killed, the other is still living.   A night or two after the
robbing of Mr. Bullock, a colored man who was passing
Allen Lowrie's called in to have a chat with him; on
going in he fell in with the whole robber gang.   They
were drinking, and some of them were drunk; now and
then one of the number would take a drink and say,
"This tastes like old Henry Bullock's brandy," which
convinced the visitor that it was their party which not
only robbed Mr. Bullock, but who were also committing all the depredations in the neighborhood.   One of
the escaped Yankee prisoners would go up to the old
man Lowrie, pat him on the head and say, "Ah, my
old gentleman, or friend, after this war is over you will
be a great general."   In this way they took advantage
of his credulity, gained his confidence, and by their
flattery led him to permit them to make his house their
headquarters, which eventually was the cause of the
old man's death.   The man who called in was badly
frightened, and made it convenient to leave as soon as
he could without exciting suspicion.

MRS. MARTHA ASHLEY.

Sometime during January or the first of February,
1865, they went to Mrs. Ashley's and demanded admittance; she inquired what they wanted; one answered
in a feminine voice, "We want your money."   She told
them they could not get it, that she had it in her pocket.

They then tried doors and windows, but failed to get in;
left to return in a few nights afterwards. Mrs. Ashley was
away from home this time, but she had a man employed to carry on her farm by the name of Paul, and
he was there. They had fallen on another plan to
effect an entrance; they hailed at the door, and Mr.
Paul inquired who it was; they answered him, saying
it was Needham Thompson (a brother of Mrs. Ashley)
and Council, (a negro belonging to her father.) Mr.
Paul opened the door, and in rushed the robber gang,
blackened and otherwise disguised, and also heavily
armed. They ransacked the house, taking off bed-
clothing, wearing apparel and anything else they could
conveniently carry. This was the first time that the
whole band entered a house in disguise. The news
spread from house to house in a few hours, and the
reign of terror, which had in some degree subsided,
again held sway over the entire community.

DAVID TOWNSEND, ESQ.

February, 1865, they entered the house of Mr.
Townsend sometime during the night, after the family
had retired. They raised a window of a back room,
which was unoccupied, and came in; they could easily
go over the house after getting in the room, as none of the
doors were locked except those on the outside. They
took a large trunk, containing all of Mr. Townsend's
valuable papers, a small amount of specie, a good
deal of Confederate money, &c. The trunk was sitting
in a room adjoining the one in which the family slept.
A hat, coat, some guns and a blanket off of one of the
beds comprised about all they took there on that visit;

they took the guns from a closet in the room where the family were sleeping. Several months afterwards the trunk was found in the woods some distance from the house; they had left the Confederate money and most of his papers in the trunk. They visited Mr. Townsend's several times after this. At one time they took his buggy-apron and harness, then went into a little out-house, where he kept his carpenter-tools and also had a bale of cotton, which they cut open, and carried off the most of his valuable tools; awhile after this they went to his black-smith shop and took a good many of his tools from there. In July, 1870, they went again; that time for provisions. Mr. Townsend, like every one else, was expecting them every night, and slept with his fire-arms at his side, all in good fix for an attack; he heard a slight noise and slipped out; he found they were trying to enter his smoke-house by boring, so as to cut out the logs. He quietly went back, prepared himself and fired upon them; they immediately returned the fire, and kept it up for sometime pretty sharply. He passed from room to room in both upper and lower stories of his dwelling and kept up a continual fire, without being exposed outside of his walls; they, on this account, being unable to locate him, fired into the house from all sides, leaving as the marks of this visit fully five hundred shot-holes. There was no one injured in the house except Mrs. Alfred Rowland, (a daughter of Mrs. Townsend) who was on a visit there at the time; she had retired and was asleep, but was aroused by the firing, and learning that they were shooting into the house, rolled off of the bed, and just as she reached the floor a spent ball struck her in the breast, and almost buried itself in the

flesh; she picked it out with her fingers, and did not suffer
any great inconvenience from it. Mr. Townsend made
a very narrow escape at one time during the fire; he
stepped out into the piazza and immediately two fired
on him, scattering the shot all around him, one ball
passing over his head, crashing the glass and lodging
in the wall beyond. He, with a renewed energy, opened
fire upon them again, when one of the gang stepped
out and called to him with an oath, to shoot—that they
were fond of such music; he fired at once to the spot
from whence the voice proceeded, and gave him the
wound that sent him in a few days to list to music less
congenial. The name of this man was said to be Gil-
berts, the murderer of young Lutterloh, of Fayetteville; he was with the gang under the assumed name of
Smith. While some of the crowd were firing, others
succeeded in entering the smoke-house, and carried off
a large lot of bacon, lard, wool, &c. There was more
than one of their party who carried off samples of Mr.
Townsend's shot on this occasion; they openly threatened to take his life, and went to his house several
times for this purpose, but he, unknown to them, had
removed to Lumberton for safety. They were seen by
some of the negroes very early one morning, soon after
Mr. T. left home, lurking around his premises; they reported it to Mrs. Townsend, and she at once dispatched
messengers to her neighbors for assistance. Several
armed themselves, mounted their horses and speedily
hastened to meet the desperadoes, but on reaching Mr.
Townsend's found all quiet; they did not enter the
house, only went up to the back gate, surveyed the
surroundings and retired. It is very probable that
some of those around the place gave them an inkling of

affairs, and they concluded that discretion was the
better part of valor this time. On their return to their
homes on that day they called at the house of Mr.
Sandy McKenzie; there was no one at the house except
Mrs. Nevin, (Mr. McKenzie's mother-in-law) and an
old black woman, those they put under guard, and ransacked the house, taking all the gentlemen's clothing
they could find. There were two young ladies from
Anson county on a visit there at the time, the Misses
Lilly, and they were out spending the day, but had left
their money concealed between the bed and mattress.
In their search they found that, and took it as a matter
of course. The last visit of the robber clan to Mr.
Townsend's was in November, 1870. Some one hailed
at the gate. Mr. Jones, a man employed at Mr. Townsend's, went out to see who it was, and found four of the
clan; they conversed with him a short time, and requested him to go in and tell Mrs. T. that they were
there, and wished to come in. He started in, they followed on and waited at the door until he should
acquaint Mrs. T. of their presence; they went in and
behaved very respectfully. They asked her for something to eat; she sent out and had supper brought into
the room where they were sitting. Henry Berry Lowrie did not eat anything, but the others, George Applewhite, Henderson Oxendine and Boss Strong ate very
heartily. Mrs. Townsend then asked them if they
wanted anything else, and they told her they would
like to have a few potatoes; she sent Mr. Jones out with
them to the potato-hill, where they had deposited their
sacks; they took about five bushels and left without further damage. They no doubt went there with far different intentions, but were completely overcome by Mrs.

Townsend's kindness. On the night of the 6th of January, 1874, Mr. Townsend's dwelling-house and kitchen were burned down, his loss amounting to between five and six thousand dollars; there is no doubt but Steve Lowrie led the party that applied the torch, as he had threatened to kill or burn out those who fed or in any way aided the men who were in search of him.

THE ROBBING OF DANIEL BAKER, McKAY SEL-
LERS, WILLIAM A. SELLERS AND MRS. DR.
NEIL McNAIR.

Those foul robberies were all committed on the same night, viz : 28th of February, A. D. 1865. The robber band on this night was composed of about thirty men. They first went to the house of Mr. Daniel Baker, who lived about two miles from the Red Bank bridge across Lumber River. Here (at Baker's) they forced their way into the main dwelling and at once commenced their di-abolical work, taking everything of value, and when they could not get keys to open locks, they broke them, bursting open trunks, drawers, &c. Not being satisfied with what they obtained in the house, they proceeded to the smoke-house and helped themselves to the finest and best bacon there. They then hitched up Mr. Baker's horse up his buggy they, and putting their plunder in the buggy proceeded up the road about four miles to the res-idence of Mr. McKay Sellers. At Mr. Sellers' they enacted the same, taking everything in his house of value. Here also they hitched Mr. Sellers' horse to his buggy, placing their plunder in the buggy. They went up the main road to Mr. William A. Sellers,' about a mile off (a brother of

Mr. McKay Sellers).   Here they arrested all the negroes
on the premises, and demanded Mr. Sellers' keys, and
put him also under arrest.   Some delay occurring in regard to finding all the keys, they proceeded to ransack
the house of Mr. Sellers, taking everything of value,
$800 in Confederate bonds and a small amount of specie.
Piling everything in front of the dwelling, they divided
the plunder among themselves, and then ordered a negro
to gear up a pair of mules to Mr. Sellers' carriage and placing everything in the carriage, they drove up the road about
half a mile to the residence of Mrs. Dr. Neil McNair, at
Argyle.   Acting here pretty much after the same manner as at other places, they ransacked the house, taking all
the valuables.   Here they were fired on by a sick Confederate soldier.   They returned the fire and acted very
roughly to the inmates of the house.   After consultation
here among themselves, the captain of the band ordered
the others to take up their line of march in the direction
of Scuffletown, inasmuch as they had as many things as
they could carry conveniently.   To Scuffletown they
went.   About sunrise next morning the vehicles that
were taken to haul off their plunder were brought back
by the negroes that were forced to go with them.

At the time these robberies were committed the Lowries were not "outlawed," and in all probability they
were led and instigated by some Yankee prisoners, who
had escaped from Florence, S. C., and made their way
into Robeson county, N. C.   Mr. William A. Sellers says
that this robbery broke him up, and did him more real
injury than Sherman's army.

THE ROBBERY OF MR. JOHN PURNELL.

In the year 1870, on the 21st of April, H. B. Lowrie, Boss Strong, Andrew Strong and George Applewhite made their appearance at the house of Mr. John Purnell, about sundown. Here they took the gun of Mr. Purnell, and ordered Mrs. Purnell to prepare supper for them, which she immediately set about doing. After they had partaken of a bountiful supper, they ransacked the house, and took everything of value, and went to the smoke-house and took therefrom about fifteen hundred pounds of meat, together with other things. At last, about ten o'clock at night, they started off with their load to Scuffletown, telling Mrs. Purnell that if she or Mr. Purnell would tell any one of their being there they would come back and kill Mr. Purnell. Many other robberies were committed about this time, such as the one committed on Mr. Peter McFarland, from whom was taken one hundred and fifty dollars in currency; Mr. Duncan McNair's smoke-house of seven or eight hundred pounds of meat; Mr. J. C. McMillan's smoke-house; Mr. John McCallum's; Mr. James H. McQueen's residence of all its valuables. But whether or not the Lowrie bandits did any or all of these outrages is unknown, inasmuch as the race of freedmen, together with the tribe, had become so demoralized that it is now a difficult task to say who committed this or that robbery, for they sympathized with each other to such an extent that no white individual knows, nor ever will.

ROBERT McKENZIE, ESQ.

It was during the month of February, 1865, that they
went to the house of this gentleman, and finding all the
doors closed and securely fastened, called loudly to Mr.
McK. for admittance.   He, with his family seated
around the fireside, gave no heed to their demands;
whereupon they burst out a panel of the door and
crowded through into the room.   They acted there in
the roughest manner, going from room to room, turning
up beds, cutting open mattresses, breaking locks, searching bureaus and trunks, behaving after the manner of
Sherman's raiders.   Failing to find money, which was
the object of their search, two of them seized Mr. Mc-
Kenzie, placed a rope around his neck, and told him if
he did not produce it they would hang him.   He told
them he had none.   They went out and consulted with
his servants, returned and in a furious manner renewed
the search, failing as before ; held another consultation
with those in the yard, came in and searched more
thoroughly, with a like result.   They turned to Mrs Mc-
Kenzie and told her if she did not give them their money
they would hang her husband, and started out with him
for this purpose; she screamed and begged them to spare
his life.   They told her then to tell them where the silver
was concealed.   She told them they had none, all the
time entreating and pleading with them, as only a wife
can plead when the life of the one who is all the world
to her is at stake.   Perhaps it was her agonizing appeals
that touched their stony hearts and caused them to desist
from their fiendish purpose.   They, too, had wives and
little ones, and it is to be hoped that, notwithstanding
their crimes, they were not wholly lost to the influence

of home affection.   After releasing Mr. McKenzie from
custody, they took his watch (a fine gold one), dishes,
knives, forks, spoons, clothing, bed-clothing and everything of value that they could carry.

When the band became disorganized from the killing
of their leader, the Federal prisoners who belonged to
the band made their escape to their Northern homes.
On their way to Wilmington one of them was conversing
with a lady on the train, and acknowledged to her that
he had been with the robber gang in Robeson county,
and, as a proof of it, showed the watch of Mr. McKenzie, which he had in his possession.

Allen Lowrie lived in less than a mile of Mr. McK.,
and continued to annoy him in almost every way possible, robbing his smoke-house, gin, pantry, cutting and
spoiling his fruit trees, grape arbors, &c.   He finally
moved away from his plantation and went to Florence,
South Carolina, where he continued to reside up to the
time of his death, in the fall of 1872.   A brother of Mr.
McKenzie took charge of his plantation in Robeson, and
fared but little better so far as robberies were concerned.
They were driving his hogs off one morning.   He followed them.   They told him to go back, but he refused.
They turned and fired on him, wounding him in the leg,
which disabled him for some time.   He finally left the
place with Mr. Phipkin in charge.   They did not trouble him so much, but he frequently met them around
the place, and they were several times at his house, but
offered no personal injury.   At one time H. B. Lowrie
hung his canteen of brandy on the fence and went off,
forgetting it.   He, however, returned in a few days
and found it where he had left, it but being very cautious, and knowing that he justly deserved death at the

hands of the Robesonians, concluded that his brandy
might possibly be drugged.   He called on Mr. P. to take
a drink before he would touch it.   Mr. P. told him it was
not poisoned unless he (H. B. L.) had done it.   He told
him he had not.   He then drank some thus setting the
fears of the outlaw at rest.

MR. DOUGALD McCALLUM.

Sometime in February, 1865, the family of Mr. McCallum were very much startled by a band of armed men
in their dwelling, numbering from eighteen to twenty—
four white men, the balance Indians.   They called for
supper, which was prepared and set for them in the
dining-room.   Before calling in all their band to supper, those that were in the house lowered the curtains of
the windows, tucking them down at the sides in order to
prevent the family from seeing and recognizing the Lowries.   After eating their supper they proceeded to search
the different rooms of the house thoroughly, throwing
the things from the windows to the party on the outside.
Here they robbed the ladies' wardrobe, an act that they
had omitted at any of their preceding visits at other
places.   The sons of Mr. McCallum were at that time
in the army, and he a gray-headed citizen, the sole protector of his wife and two daughters.   They took his
clothing, guns, and seven hundred dollars in Confederate money, which was almost valueless, it being a short
time before the surrender.   A lot of clothing, bed-clothing and a purse of silver comprised the balance of their
booty on this occasion.   They had a quarrel over the
silver in the yard before leaving.   After their search
was completed they prepared to convey away their

gains by going to the horse-lot and harnessing two horses to separate buggies, and removed the things to some place of deposit, and continued their raid by visiting the houses of Messrs. John McCallum and Robert Graham.

MR. JOHN McCALLUM.

They reached this place about **11** o'clock. **Mr.** McCallum and his niece were the only white people on the premises, and the first intimation they had of the presence of this marauding party was the report of a pistol on the front piazza of their dwelling. The yard dog felt the effects of this, as he was found dead the next morning on the piazza. They called loudly to Mr. McCallum to open the door, threatening him in a rough manner; he very reluctantly admitted them, about thirty in number, as near as he could guess. They stationed a guard at every door, and the parlor was crowded with them. The white men told Mr. McC. that they were escaped Federal prisoners. They would only allow a dim light, and when that would chance to fall on their faces, they would immediately drop their blankets over them. They were very profane, and showed no respect for age or sex. They thoroughly searched the house, upper and lower story, emptied all the bureaus and trunks, taking every key on the place. They did not leave a change of wearing apparel, and scarcely any bed-clothing. Two guns, and nearly everything else of value that could be carried off conveniently, were taken. After they completed their search

a few of the party went down to Mr. Robert Graham's,
taking a horse and buggy, with one of the negroes to drive
it, and the balance remained there until their return.
They came back before day and demanded of Mr. Mc-
Callum his money and brandy.   He told them that he
did not have any; whereupon, they cursed and threatened to kill him if he did not produce it.   They compelled him to accompany them to his gin-house, taking
with them a lighted candle to search in the cotton for it.
They would make him dig down in the cotton while they
stood sticking the burning candle to it.   He begged them
not to burn it, and kept trying to assure them that he
had neither money nor brandy.   The negro boy who
had accompanied the party to Mr. Graham's told them
that his master had something concealed in his gin-house,
and he thought it money and brandy; for this reason
they renewed the search on their return.   Meeting with
no success, and it then being nearly daylight, they took
their departure, still retaining the negro, horse and buggy in their service.   The boy returned in a few hours,
but was too much intoxicated to tell anything about it.

Mr. John Purcell lived about a half mile from Mr.
McCallum's, on their direct route home, and in passing
there T. C. Bridgers was standing on the piazza, and
they saluted him by firing a pistol into the house, the
ball passing just over his head.   They never at any time
entered the dwelling of Mr. Purcell, but his gin, store
and smoke-house were robbed several times by the gang.
They were often seen in the day lurking arounnd his
plantation.   Mr. P., in the spring of 1862, came upon
Steve Lowrie asleep in the corner of the fence, with his
gun standing a short distance from him. This was near the
house of a family of Indians, who were Mr. Purcell's

tenants. Steve, no doubt, was waiting for his breakfast, as the family were known to not only cook and wash for him, but also to give the band all the information they could gather. They were near relatives of the Strongs and Lowries. The same day that Mr. Purcell saw Steve Lowrie, he, with Andrew Strong, went to the house of Mr. Henry McCallum, a son of Mr. John Mc-Callum, and took his gun and watch. Mrs. McCallum asked them to give her the watch, and they did it.

Thus for years they continued to roam the country, day and night, plundering, dropping in here and there when least expected. The citizens were afraid to let more than one or two at a time into a plan to capture them; the friends of the gang were so numerous, scattered throughout the country, that it was impossible to make a move without their becoming apprised of it. Their friends were as loud in denunciation of them as their enemies; for this reason it was impossible in many cases to discover between the two.

MR. ROBERT GRAHAM.

When the party, fifteen or twenty in number, which left Mr. McCallum's for Mr. Graham's, reached there it was between twelve and four o'clock in the morning. They immediately posted sentinels in and around the yard, and on every road leading to the house, with instructions to allow no one to pass in, out, or advance from any direction. These warlike orders were issued and obeyed with promptness. Some of the band—three whites, the other Indians—rushed into the piazza of the dwelling, and with loud oaths and threats demanded admittance.

None of the family were at home except Mr. Graham
and his daughter.   He went to the door and asked who
it was and what they wanted.   They replied with hor-
rid oaths for him to open the door, saying if he did not
they would set fire to his house.   Hearing this awful
threat, he opened the door; they went in, at once making him prisoner, at the same time demanding his guns,
ammunition, and every key on the place.   This demand
was made by a white man, who termed himself Captain.
After getting the guns and keys in possession, they
lighted their candles, with which they seemed to be well
supplied, and proceeded to plunder and ransack the house
of many valuables.   In this they seemed to be well dis-
ciplined, as they would take according to rank, viz:
Captain, first of the most valuable articles, and so on.
The three white men, being all officers, had the best of
the spoils, consisting of money to the amount of two
thousand dollars, a purse of silver, a watch which Mr.
Graham prized very highly, having worn it from boy-
hood, several pieces of jewelry belonging to different
members of the family, and also the rings from Miss
Graham's fingers.   The privates all being well supplied
with large bags and haversacks, took wearing apparel
of every description, bed-clothing, boots, shoes, hats, &c.
After they had completed their search they ordered supper to be prepared immediately, with directions how
and what to prepare; they then ordered Mr. Graham
and his daughter to take seats in the parlor for their entertainment.   None were allowed to enter except the
officers, the privates being left out in the cold, who, by
the way, seemed highly elated over the spoils they had
captured.   After some time spent in asking Mr. Graham
(the old man, as they called him) many questions about

his sons in the army, war matters and the "rebs" gener- ally, they told him that he or his daughter had to go with them as prisoners of war. This they possitively refued to hear, when some of the officers proposed to take them by force, and put a handkerchief around Miss Graham's neck for this purpose, when the Captain with a millitary air, ordered that no violence should be used. To this they quietly yielded. Finding that their time (night) was limited, they issued orders to prepare to leave, not waiting for supper, as they had counter- manded their orders to have it prepared. This was supposed to have been done for fear that some of the servants would recognize their colored soldiery, which was afterwards found to be true.

On leaving they went to the smoke-house and helped themselves to the largest bacon hams they could find. Here the Captain again interfered, saying: "Boys, we have done enough here, let us go." They took one or two hams, and said they would be back in a few nights for a large supply of bacon and corn. They made ready to leave, which was to Mr. Graham the most agreeable part of their night's proceedings. In bidding them good night, the Captain handed Mr. Graham one of his guns, first discharging it, then breaking the rammer and throwing the flint away, saying: "Take this old man, it will do to shoot the robbers with; they are becoming very troublesome these war times, and everybody should be prepared for them." After this piece of advice, they left for headquarters, then in Back Swamp.

CALVIN OXENDINE.

On evidence of John Dial, a member of the robber

clan, but who turned State's evidence against the clan,
Calvin was arrested and lodged in Wilmington jail with
Steve Lowrie and George Applewhite, as one of their
number, at the time of the robbery and murder of ex-
Sheriff King. Calvin refused to leave jail with them at
the time of their escape, alleging afterwards as his reason, that he was innocent and would be proven so on
trial. He being cousin to the outlaws, did not believe
that he could get a fair trial in Robeson, his native county, where all their bloody scenes were enacted; it was
therefore removed to Southport, in Brunswick county,
where he proved an alibi by a gentleman from Richmond county, in whose employ he had been, and was at
the time of the said robbery and murder. He also
proved by the same gentleman so good a character for
honest industry that the evidence of the notorious Dial was
discredited by the jury, and consequently a verdict of
"not guilty" was rendered, and he was acquitted.

He was brother to Henderson Oxednine, the only outlaw that died on the gallows.

MR. DANIEL BAKER SHOT.

On November 18th, 1866, (Monday night) the Lowrie
bandits visited the house of Mr. Daniel Baker, who resided about two miles from Red Banks Bridge across
Lumber river. Here they commenced plundering, taking cotton from his cotton house, &c. Mr. Baker dis-
covering them, ordered them away, whereupon they
fired on him, shattering the bones in his right leg so ter-
ribly that amputation had to be resorted to in order to
to save his life, which was successfully accom-

plished soon after the occurrence by Dr. W. D. McCallum, the family physician.   Now this act of the Lowrie bandits was nothing more nor less than wanton cruelty, inasmuch as Mr. Baker was their neighbor and friend. A more industrious, hard-working, clever and kind-hearted man could not be found in the county than was Mr. Daniel Baker, yet this act of the Lowrie bandits made him a cripple for life, and hastened doubtless his earthly career, for he suffered much pain ever afterwards until death released him from his sufferings.

MR. ANGUS S. BAKER.

On the 1st of November, 1871, the Lowrie robbers went into the residence of Mr. Angus S. Baker, broke to his house about 9 o'clock p. m., arrested Mr. Baker and wife, and ransacked the house, taking beds, bedding, blankets and wearing apparel, in short, everything of value they could find, and left about 2 o'clock a. m., with their plunder, for Scuffletown.

MR. MALLOY McPHAUL.

In the year 1868, the robber clan would sometimes employ artifice to gain access into dwellings to obtain such articles of food or clothing as they deemed necessary.   As an instance of their cunning I give the following particulars of a visit by them to Mr. McPhaul's : A white man, appearing to be a traveler, called at his house and told him he was from Whiteville, (the county-seat of an adjoining county, where a brother of Mr. McPhaul resided); that his brother was at the point of

death, and desired him to go down immediately if he
wished to see him alive.   Mr. McPhaul made arrangements to take the first train ; arriving at his brother's,
what was his surprise at finding him in excellent health;
he at once understood the ruse that had been employed
at his expense; with a mind filled with dread forebod-
ings and distracting fear, not knowing to what indignity
his family had been subjected, he hastened back home.
He was, however, much relieved to find them unhurt,
although the robbers had been there in his absence.
After he was fairly on his way to his brother's a party
of three men went to his house and demanded the keys
of the smoke house of his wife, which she refused to give
them, but offered to unlock the door for them, to which
they consented.   They took bacon and other articles
of food, then left without further molestation.

THE MURDER OF EX-SHERIFF REUBEN KING.

On the night of the 23rd of January, 1869, the quiet
little village of Lumberton, in Robeson county, was
thrown into consternation by the startling intelligence
that Sheriff Reuben King had been shot in his own house
(one and one-half miles from Lumberton) by the Lowrie gang, afterwards known as the outlaws.   The gang
at this time was composed of Stephen, Thomas and
Henry Berry Lowrie, Andrew and Boss Strong, George
Applewhite, Shoemaker John, William Chavis, Henderson and Calvin Oxendine, Zack McLauchlin and John
Dial.

They had been concealed near the house all day,
watching for Sheriff King.   Late in the afternoon King

returned from the village, and while seated at his fireside, part of the band entered his house with the intention (it is supposed) of robbing the Sheriff. Henry Berry, who led the van, approached him with his gun presented, and demanded of the Sheriff his money. Had he complied with the bandit's demand, his life would probably have been spared; but King instantly sprang up and seized the gun of the robber chief, and refused to give up his money. It has been admitted that the intention of the gang was merely to get money, and not to kill the Sheriff. The impression was that he had a large amount of money on his person or in his house, but they were sadly disappointed, as will be shown hereafter.

In the scuffle that ensued between the robber chieftain and the Sheriff, the gun was discharged, the contents passing through the floor. George Applewhite, who was standing on the piazza, near the door, rushed to the rescue of his comrade by firing a navy revolver at King, the ball taking effect in his back, under the right shoulder blade, lodging in the lung. Mr. S. E. Ward, a neighbor, was on a visit to the family for the night, and at the time the shooting occurred, was sitting by the fire near a table. He arose from his seat and raised his arm, when John Dial fired at him, the load of shot taking effect in his arm and side, inflicting a very painful, though not dangerous wound. They then proceeded to search the house; breaking open trunks, drawers, &c., carrying off a large quantity of wearing apperal, bedclothing and other articles, many of which were afterwards found in George Applewhite's house and identified as those taken the night of the wounding of the Sheriff. Some of the bed clothing was produced as evi-

dence in the subsequent trial of the parties for the murder of Sheriff King, and indeed was one of the strongest
links in the evidence against them. The robbers had
disguised themselves by blacking their faces, &c., and
consequently escaped detection by the family or Mr. W.
Taking advantage of the confusion and fright their appearance and outrages had occasioned, they made well
their escape.

Physicians were immediately summoned, who care-
fully examined the wounded men, and pronounced Mr.
Ward's case not at all serious, but not so Sheriff King's.
The deadly weapon in the hands of the fell assassin had
made sure its aim and entered a vital part. The
wounds of the Sheriff were found to be mortal. With
blanched cheeks and agonized hearts, relatives and
and friends received this decision of the physicians. The
fiat had gone forth—Sheriff King must die; he would
live a month, perhaps six weeks. He lingered seven
weeks and died, such a death!—by the hands of a
band of desperadoes, in the midst of his family, and at
his own hearth. Ah! methinks if there is punishment
greater meted out to one than to another, it will certainly
be inflicted on those midnight assasins who committed
crimes of the blackest dye.

Every effort was made to capture the murderers, but
without success. The dense swamps of Robeson county
(impenetrable to all save the outlaws) afforded them
protection from justice for some time. After a while,
however, Henry Berry Lowrie was prevailed upon to
surrender to Sheriff Howell and Dr. Thomas, Agent of
the Freedmen's Bureau. John Dial was arrested by
Deputy Sheriff McDonald. George Applewhite was ar-

rested at Red Banks; Shoemaker John was also arrested, and Dial became State's evidence in the murder
of ex-Sheriff King. Stephen Lowrie, Calvin and Henderson Oxendine were also arrested and confined in Wilmington jail, tried, convicted and sentenced to be
hanged; but an appeal was taken to the Supreme Court.
As is often the case, before the decision of said appeal,
Henry Berry and Steve Lowrie, George Applewhite,
Henderson and Calvin Oxendine effected an escape
from jail and took up their abode in the swamps of Robeson county—thence arose the band of outlaws. Their
escape from the Wilmington jail is, and ever will remain,
enveloped in mystery to those outside of the parties who
aided and abetted them. The jail, it must be remembered, was a very strong one, closely guarded, and the
jailer residing within its walls, though this is only one
of the many mysteries connected with the proceedings
of the "Lowrie Band."

After Sheriff King was wounded he removed his money from his pocket, placing it under the collar of his
coat, to prevent the robbers from getting it. He was
detected in the act by one of the robbers, and they succeeded in getting about $155 in currency and $20 in
gold. At the time they were searching the house, the
Sheriff was lying in the door beseeching some one to
give him water. The family had left the premises
through fright, and not one of that merciless band would
gratify his request, but heaped curses and abuses on
him, telling him that he ought to have died long ago, &c.

HENRY BULLOCK, SR.

In May, 1869, early in the evening, Mr. Bullock was
surprised by several men disguised as negroes coming

into his field where he was superintending his farm
hands. He was an aged veteran of the war of 1812,
and though he was ninety-five years of age at the time
of their visit, was able to attend to his farm. One of
the clan walked up to the old man, and, notwithstanding
his age and feebleness, jerked him around, ordering him
to go to the house and give them his money. He told them
he had no money, but could go to the house with them.
On their way they had to cross a fence, but did not allow the decrepit old man to get over the fence, but
pushed him over. When they got to the house they ordered the old gentleman and his wife to go in, and left
his laborers under guard in the yard. They arrested all
who chanced to pass the house while they were there,
and kept them under guard until they left In their
search they found thirty dollars ($30) in specie belong-
ing to Mrs. Bullock, which they appropriated. They
carried off all of his valuable papers, clothing, bed-
clothing and provisions to a large amount. They found
a jug of brandy in the house, and before they would
drink any themselves. compelled the old lady to drink a
glass of it pure. They, no doubt, thought it was drugged,
and used this precaution to ascertain. They cursed the
old people in a shocking manner. You, reader, can picture in your own imagination, after reading this one
short sketch, the character of the gang with whom the
people of Robeson had to contend. Age and decrepi-
tude could claim no mercy at their hands, but regardless
of all -- reckless of all save their own inordinate love of
plunder, they rose up, sometimes in one place to-day,
ten miles hence to-morrow, casting a shadow, throwing
a gloom around many a hearth-stone in a large portion
of Robeson.

MR. DAVID McKELLAR.

In May, 1869, the robber clan visited the house of Mr. McKellar, in his absence, and took three hundred and fifty dollars ($350) and some clothing.

MR. M. K. GRIFFIN.

This was the next house they visited in that neighborhood; they were also in disguise, and armed with double-barreled guns. They rushed into the yard with guns presented, and took Mr. Griffin prisoner, at once demanding his money, cursing and using very abusive language towards him. There were only three at his house; they searched his person, placed one of their number to guard him, while the other two proceeded to search the house. They took all of his and his wife's most valuable clothing and his gun; they afterwards threw the gun into the garden and left it. They inquired of Mr. G. about his neighbors, the number of men about the different houses, their strength of arms, &c. When they started off, they turned to Mr. G. with an oath, and told him to stay at home that night, or they would see him again if he did not. The wife of Mr. Griffin was so badly frightened that she never recovered from the effects of it.

MR. GEORGE WILLIAMS.

In the year A. D. 1869, the robber gang went to Mr. Geo. Williams' and broke a door down that was on the front side of the house, and fired at one of his sons, but did not hit him. The family fled, and left the house and

its contents in their hands; they, however, took nothing
off. The firing at young Mr. Williams seemed to have
been merely venting their ire on account of some old
grudge.

MR. WILLIAM C. McNEILL.

Among the many families harassed by the "Lowrie
Band" there were few that suffered to the same extent
as Mr. W. C. McNeill, one of Robeson's most quiet, inof-
fensive and law-abiding citizens. Living as he did on
the very borders of their settlement, he was more frequently subjected to their insults and depredations than
those more distant, and being also a well-to-do farmer,
his larder and farm-yard possessed for them great at-
tractions. Mr. McNeill had also incurred their marked
displeasure by freely expressing his opinion, and treating
with the utmost contempt this band and all that he knew
to be its friends.

Their first visit to his house was in 1869, at which
time they entered his pantry and dining-room, relieving
them of all available articles and eatables, which was to
Mr. McNeill and family a considerable loss. This act of
lawlessness supplied their homes with many useful articles, and themselves with many necessaries and luxuries.

In the early part of 1870 they again entered his dining-room (which had been refurnished) and stripped it as
before of every available article. On this visit they attempted an entrance to his smoke-house by digging un-
derneath it and trying to open it with false keys (having
a goodly number of them), but failing to effect an entrance here, they quietly left, no doubt to attempt it
somewhere else.

One night in 1862, Mr. McNeill was out walking in his lane. Hearing footsteps in the direction of his barn, and suspecting who they were, he hastily concealed himself in order to learn their intentions; immediately one man walked to the barn and endeavored to open it. Mr. McNeill called out twice to know who they were; receiving no answer, he told them if they did not leave, he would force them to; one answered, "Do you know to whom you are talking?" Recognizing the voice, he made no reply, but returned to the house, took his gun, and again went out; they in the meantime had left the barn and repaired to a corner of the fence nearer the house; as Mr. McNeill walked out they halted him; he again asked "Who are you?" One, with an oath, cried out, "It is Lowrie."

Mr. McNeill at once commenced retracing his steps into the house, when they fired at him; the contents of the gun passed him, lodging in the breast of his beautiful daughter and accomplished wife, inflicting painful though not dangerous wounds. Mrs. McNeill and her daughter were standing on the piazza anxiously watching the husband and father when the shot was fired. On the following day Henry Berry Lowrie visited Moss Neck, a depot on the Carolina Central Railway, and within a few hundred yards of Mr. McNeill's residence; he denied all knowledge of the shooting, and expressed great indignation at the guilty parties for having shot two ladies; he sent for Mr. McNeill to go to the depot; he wanted to tell him that he did not do it, but he (Mr. McNeill) refused to see or to have anything to say to him.

On the next day he again visited Moss Neck, and was under the influence of liquor; he seemed to be excited,

and several times asserted that he did shoot at Mr. Mc-
Neill and tried his best to kill him.

Their visits to this family did not cease, frequently
they made raids on their fowl-house, helping themselves
lavishly to all it contained.   On their return from one
of these raids they called at Mr. Dougald McCormick's,
passing themselves for a squad of men in search of the
outlaws, and requested him to accompany them; he,
not being satisfied as to their identity, made some ex-
cuse to remain at home; they then gave him a bucket,
demanding some flour; he gave them some, and they
went off, making no further demands.

THE MURDER OF MR. O. C. NORMENT.

On the night of the 19th of March, A. D. 1870, a
quarter to 9 o'clock, Mr. Norment was shot in his yard,
only a few feet from the door.   The party who committed this deed had stationed themselves at each corner of the house, and had entered the yard by taking
down the palings of the enclosure, just large enough for
one man to crawl through at a time.   I suppose the family would have heard the noise of the drawing out of the
palings had it not been for the noise of the children
frolicking with their father at the time.   Circumstances
seemed to favor them on this occasion.   With the laughter of innocence ringing in their ears, they took their
positions to commit the deed so horrible to relate. Mr. Norment was in the habit of putting his children to sleep by
telling them little nursery stories, and took them to the bed
nearest the murderer for this purpose, little thinking so
soon his home would be made desolate, and the place

desecrated, yet made memorable to his stricken family
by the life-blood of the husband and father.   The fiend
who stood there and listened to the merry laughter and
innocent prattle of his little ones, with the dark purpose
in his heart of taking from them their kind and loving
father in so cruel a manner, must have had a heart of
adamant, or he would have yielded to the gentle influence, and turned from so bad a design.   But no; he stood
there nursing the resolve that would blacken his soul
with crime, and doom him to a punishment as only such
criminals merit at the hands of an avenging God.   After the children were quietly slumbering, he arose and
took a seat by the fire, conversing for a short time, when
he remarked to his wife, in a low tone, that he heard a
noise.   She replied that she had dropped a hair-pin on
the hearth, and supposed that was the noise he heard.
He said no, it was not that, but expressed no uneasiness.   In a short time he opened the door and stepped
out, leaving it open.   His wife was looking out at the
door and saw the flash of the gun pass.   Simultaneously
he groaned, and she sprang to the door screaming; she
has no recollection of hearing the report of the gun.   When
she saw the flash of the gun, she comprehended in an
instant the situation of her husband, but thought that he
had been shot down in the yard, and her intention was
to get to him; but he had not fallen.   After going into
the yard he thought he heard a footstep, and turned to
go in the house, when they fired; he leaped to the door,
where he was met by his wife just in the act of falling,
when she caught and pulled him into the house.   He
whispered to her to close and fasten the door, and hand
him his rifle, as they might attempt to enter and complete their bloody work.   She did as he desired, and

kneeling by him, supported him, in order that he might
have both hands in the use of his gun, and in case they
entered, he might at least kill one. She continued
screaming until her father (Mr. J. D. Bridgers), with several members of his family, got there. On getting to the
door and finding it fastened, they called to her to open
it. Knowing her support was necessary to the comfort
of her husband, she replied she could not; whereupon,
they burst it open and rushed in, finding them in the situation described. They at once inquired of Mr. Norment how he did it, thinking he accidentally wounded
himself. He soon explained. Mr. J. D. Bridgers and
his son, John Bridgers, started in pursuit of the perpe-
trators; they had only gone a short distance when Mr.
Norment requested some one present to go and tell them
to return, as they were risking their lives without a probability of coming up with them. They returned, and after
placing Mr. N. in a more comfortable position and
binding up the wound, one of his brothers-in-law (J. T.
Bridgers) started for Dr. John Dick, who lived about four
miles distant, at the same time dispatching a negro boy
for Dr. R. M. Norment, a brother of Mr. Norment, who
was also a physician, living in Lumberton, a distance of
fourteen miles. When they were momentarily expecting
the arrival of Dr. Dick, they were again startled by the
loud report of a gun in less than a mile on the road
which the doctor would come. The family were fearful that they had fired on the doctor to prevent his coming to the sufferer's relief. After a lapse of about an
hour and a half, the doctor came, accompanied by J. F.
and T. C. Bridgers, reporting that three-fourths of a
mile above the house a man stepped from behind a tree
and shot the mule; that they jumped out, in their haste

and excitement leaving the medicine in the buggy. As
they crossed the road to the opposite side from where
the man was standing who did the shooting, they passed
in arm's length of two others. A negro, who was at the
house of Mr. Norment when the doctor came, volunteer-
ed to go for the medicine if Mr. Bridgers would lend him
a gun. The gun was furnished, and he, with three others,
started after the medicines. A short distance from the
house of Mr. Norment, one of the negroes stated that he
saw a woman, or man dressed in women's clothes, run
from the road into the bushes. The supposition was
that it was either the wife or mother of some one of the
number who did the shooting at Mr. Norment's. The
negroes returned just before daylight with the medicines,
reporting the mule dead, and the parties near the place,
as they had distinctly heard voices close by. They no
doubt expected John Bridgers to go for the medicine,
and in case that he did they would murder him also,
as they openly declared that it was their intention to
shoot both Mr. Norment and John Bridgers on that
night They had both been very active in attempting
the capture of the murderers of ex-Sheriff King, and for
thus transgressing the assumed rights of the murderous
gang their lives were to be the forfeit. Drs. R. F.
Lewis and R. M. Norment reached Mr. Norment's
about 4 o'clock in the morning. They, with the assistance of Drs. Dick and Barnes, proceeded to examine the
wound, and pronounced amputation necessary, as the
bones of the right leg were completely shattered. About
5 o'clock in the afternoon the operation was completed,
and Mr. N. was found to be in almost a dying condition,
from which he revived for a few hours. From the
shock, loss of blood, and the use of chloroform, all com-

bined, reaction never took place, and he expired a
quarter to 7 o'clock the morning of the 21st, living
about thirty-six hours after he was wounded.

This diabolical deed spread gloom and terror throughout the community, and may well be said to have been
the beginning of the war in Robeson county with the
Lowrie Banditti.   For weeks and months the citizens of
this county slept with their guns by their sides; the
young men, armed and equipped, went forth in search
of the vile desperadoes; with steady tramp and hushed
voices they traversed the country for miles, but with
little or no success.

I will here state the true causes which led to the shooting of Mr. Norment.   After the surrender he was com-
missioned captain of the militia.   The robber clan had
then been operating in the county about two years, robbing and plundering at their pleasure—unmolested.
After the murder of Sheriff King, Mr. Norment received
orders to take out a portion of the militia and endeavor
to capture his murderers, which he did, but was unsuccessful.   He also had orders to arrest Zack McLaughlin
on the charge of stealing.   On taking him to trial, sufficient evidence not being elicited against him, he was released.   Although he knew Mr. Norment acted under orders, it did not tend to quell the revengeful ire of his nature, and he determined to kill him.   Sometime prior to
this Andrew Strong had been arrested by Mr. N. for robbing the gin-house of Mr. John Purcell; he was also released on the same grounds.   These two were the principal
actors in this deed of blood, urged on by others of their
friends.

Mr. Norment was a mechanic by trade.   Those in the
vicinity where he lived can testify to his usefulness.

MR. JAMES D. BRIDGERS.

A few weeks after the murder of Mr. Norment four of
the robber clan were discovered making an entrance into the enclosure of Mr. Bridgers; two of his sons, John
and A. C. Bridgers, fired on them from the windows,
and they hastily retired without doing any damage.
They were often around the premises for the purpose,
as they afterwards declared, of shooting his sons above
named, as they had been active in attempting their capture.   For this purpose they visited his house on the
17th of August, 1870, after dark; they made various
noises around the yard, hoping to draw them out, but
they did not succeed.   The Messrs. Bridgers know
ing the superiority of the number of the gang (about
fifteen) with   whom   they   had   to   contend,   and
hearing them at different points around the yard, kept
within doors, impatiently waiting for them to come in
closer quarters.   The robber gang having been informed
that their opponents here were well prepared to meet them,
and that they would have bloody work should they ever
enter the yard, concluded on this occasion to satiate
their thirst for blood, and also to vent their spite in another quarter. Zack McLaughlin remarked to the gang,
"Well, boys, we have come to-night for blood, and must
not be disappointed, we'll shoot the old man's cattle."
According, they passed on to the cow-lot, and commenced shooting in a shocking manner the harmless
brutes.   The Messrs. Bridgers fired on them from the
house, but the night being extremely dark, could only
tell of their whereabouts by the flash of their guns; they
fired only a few times after the boys opened on them;
they then retired, leaving two cows shot down and sev-

eral others badly wounded. This cruel, inhuman act
shows in a proper light the character of the fiends with
whom the people of Robeson had to contend.

Just after the robbers commenced firing on the cattle,
the family learned from the simultaneous flashing of their
guns that their number was more than they at first an-
ticipated. They concluded to blow the trumpet, hoping
that some of their neighbors might hear and come to their
aid; as soon as the first sound of the trumpet rent the
air, the robbers fired more rapidly, fiercely yelling, at
the same time the dogs barking, and the firing going on
from the house making quite a discordant sound. The
excitement for a short time is past description. Their
next visit to Mr. Bridgers' was on the 14th day of July, 1871,
the same day on which they sent Mr. McNair with the
letter to Col. Sinclair and Sheriff McMillan, ordering the
release of their wives, who were kept in confinement
in Lumberton, for the purpose, as it is said, of "starving
out the outlaws." Such a thing, though, was preposter-
ous, for they certainly had many friends, white and colored, that aided them at any time and in any way desired. They came to Mr. Bridgers' about 12 o'clock;
they ate dinner, and conducted themselves very quietly.
Steve Lowrie did not come until after the others had
eaten; he came up picking his "banjo" and singing,
seemed in excellent spirits. The five desperadoes, heavily armed with repeaters, bowie-knives, double-barreled
guns and Spencer rifles, until they were burdensome to
carry, formed really a formidable looking party. They
all started to meet Mr. McNair about 4 o'clock in the
afternoon; they did not go far before they met him; he
delivered them Col. Sinclair's reply, which seemed in
no wise to suit their wishes. With an angry scowl they

perused each line, and the deep, dark anger which settled in their faces reminded one of the heavy mutterings
that precede the thunder storm, and, no doubt, would
have fallen in all its fury on many an innocent head
but for the timely interposition of some of our grey-
headed citizens, who succeeded in getting those in
authority to release the wives of the desperadoes. The
last visit of the entire band to Mr. Bridgers' was in
August, 1871. Several of the neighbors were there
working on his gins; among them was Mr. Thomas Bullard, whom H. B. Lowrie had determined to kill; he
went there on this occasion, as he openly avowed to a
gentleman on his way, for this purpose. The cause of
his animosity to Mr. B. was this: He, in company with
Boss Strong, had met Messrs. Bullard and Holcomb a
few days before, and gave them positive commands not
to mention seeing them to any one; they mentioned it to
some one, and it finally reached the ears of Henry Berry,
and for this reason only he determined to kill him. He
told Mr. Bullard to walk with him a short distance, as he
wanted to talk with him privately; they walked off about
a hundred yards and sat down; in a few minutes some
of the young men followed, and learned that H. B. Lowrie was very much enraged with Mr. B., and that his
anger must in some way be appeased, or another victim
would also be added to the list already on record against
him.   The gentlemen were unarmed, and therefore
helpless to give any aid by force of arms; two of the
gentlemen present affirmed that they had been with Mr.
B. the day after he had seen H. B. L., and he did not
mention seeing him at all, and that he had been misin-

formed, &c. This quieted him somewhat, and he concluded to release him for the present, provided he would be more careful in the future.

MR. ZACH FULMORE.

On the third Sabbath in May, 1870, they went to the house of Mr. Fulmore during the absence of the family at church. There was a negro left in charge of the house, and he had fallen asleep; he was aroused from his nap by four armed men in disguise. They went into the dwelling, broke open trunks, drawers, &c., ransacked the house, and carried off a large amount in valuable articles and money. Mr. Robert Chaffin and wife were on a visit to Mr. Fulmore at the time, but had also gone to church, leaving their trunk there; this they entered, taking a suit of Mr. Chaffin's, a watch-case, key and some very valuable papers that were in the trunk. They did not trouble Mrs. Chaffin's clothing beyond robbing the pocket of a dress of a small pen-knife.

ALEXANDER McMILLAN, ESQ.

On Sunday morning, 12th of September, 1870, five of these desperadoes made their appearance at the house of Mr. McMillan. The Messrs. McMillan were at the gin-house near the dwelling, engaged in making a coffin for a child of one of their neighbors, when they approached them in their usual disguise as negroes. They at once took them prisoners and marched them into the kitchen, placed them under guard of one of their number, while the others searched the house. Breakfast

for the family was on the table, to which their guard
quietly helped himself. They robbed the house of a
large quantity of bed-clothing, wearing apparel, guns,
pistols, and five dollars in money. They presented a
gun at the breast of Mr. Alexander McMillan, and cursed both him and his sister in a shameful manner. The
Messrs. McMillan had been expecting a visit from the
robbers for some time, and were in the constant habit
of keeping their guns with them, but it being the Sabbath day, omitted their usual precaution. The robbers
no doubt had been watching their opportunity, and took
advantage of their separation from their arms that morning to put their plans into execution. They rushed first
into the house and got possession of their guns and pistols, and then there was no difficulty in deterring them
from anything like resistance. They came after this,
and robbed his smoke-house of four or five hundred
pounds of bacon. The Messrs. McMillan discovered
them at another time inside their enclosure, and fired
upon them; the robbers returned the fire without any
damage. Scarcely a week passed up to this time without some citizen of Robeson being robbed; no matter
how cautious, watchful and circumspect the people
were, at an unwary hour the fiends would suddenly
fall upon them, and before they could realize their situation or prepare for defense, have them unarmed and
helpless, unable to raise a hand in defense of their
homes.

ROBBERY OF MR. E. H. PAUL.

Thursday the 4th day of August, 1870, dawned bright
and beautiful. The sun shot up from beyond the

eastern horizon, and shone as it were with increased
brilliancy, and "nature in her glory smiled." That day
was to decide the great political contest between the
two parties of North Carolina. The last month had
been one of great excitement, and was said to have witnessed the liveliest campaign that had ever taken place
in the State, but it was over; the speakers had retired
from the field, and all was quiet. Every effort had
been made by the good people of Robeson county to
throw off the yoke of Radical tyranny that had been for
the past five years galling them so bitterly. Here the
true citizens were fully aroused to their duty, as well as
interest, and resolved to discharge that duty, they
went to the polls determined to elect good men men
that would adhere strictly to a just administration of
the law, and aid them in bringing to justice the band of
murderers that cut off so many of her best men, and re-
store the peace and quiet of former years.

These dastardly thieves, taking advantage of the necessary absence of the voters from their homes, planned
and perpetrated one of the coolest and most daring robberies that ever shocked a community. While Mr. E.
H. Paul, a young man who then resided in Alfordsville
Township, and who owned a store and turpentine dis-
tillery, was absent at the polls, they went to his house
and demanded of his sister the key that opened the
store; she having thrown it away when she saw them
coming, replied that she did not have it; whereupon
they arrested her and her cousin, Mr. Richard Paul,
and all the domestics, put them in the kitchen, placed a
guard at the door, and proceeded to the store. One
of the party (who was afterwards ascertained to have
been Saunders, the detective) took a key from his pocket

and opened the door. They then seized such things as
they wanted, which consisted of dry goods and grocer-
ies, to a large amount. Taking the mule and cart of
Davis Bullard (who had arrived while they were plundering, and had been put with others under guard), they
conveyed their booty to some place where it was received by their allies and conveyed away; returning the
mule and cart, they coolly took their departure. Steve
Lowrie was recognized as one of the plundering party
by one of those placed under guard.

ROBBERY OF MRS. WILLIAM McKAY.

On the 3rd day of October, A. D. 1870, the whole
band of outlaws, together with four other men, all
blacked and disguised, made their appearance at the
residence of Mrs. William McKay, near Floral College,
in the hope of finding Mr. John Taylor there, as he had
spoken of going to Mrs. McKay's to live, she being his sister; and as he had been recently burnt out at Moss
Neck by the outlaws, they supposed that he had already
moved, but in this they were disappointed; Mr. John
Taylor was not there. Six of the number were stationed
outside of the yard, whilst the other five rushed in at
the gate, shooting a large Newfoundland dog as they
went along. Entering the main residence they went
through where the family of Mrs. McKay were at the
time. On seeing them, Mrs. McKay ran to see where
her children were. The outlaws ordered her to stop,
bringing their guns to bear upon her; she told them that
she only wanted to gather her children up, as any good
mother would have done. They then put the family

under arrest. the negroes fleeing in every direction. Leaving one of their number to guard Mrs. McKay and family, the rest commenced ransacking the house, first taking the jewelry, then every other thing of value, including bed-clothes and wearing apparel. After getting through, they told Miss Pattie McKay (a step-daughter of Mrs. McKay) that she must play some on the piano-forte for them, which she did, in order to keep them in a good humor; after she finished playing for them one of them told her that she had a gold ring on her finger which he wanted, and that she must give it up; she readily pulled the ring off and tossed it to him, remarking that he was cruel. Considering that the outlaws were just from the brandy still of Mr. Angus Leach, a near neighbor of Mrs. McKay's, and had taken a considerable quantity of brandy from the still, and considering, too, that they all loved brandy, and that a goodly number of them were drunk, it is surprising that they behaved as well as they did at Mrs. McKay's; they offered no insult to either her or family, except arresting and holding them under arrest until they had plundered her house; they remarked to her on leaving that they needed everything that they had taken, that they had to live as well as other people, etc.

Reader, imagine a highly cultivated widow lady, with her two little boys and an accomplished step-daughter, under the arrest of drunken outlaws, and you have the situation! Some time elapsed after the outlaws left Mrs. McKay's ere she could get a negro to carry a note to one of her neighbors, informing them of her situation. How true it is that no one knows what a day may bring forth.

THE OLD FIELD FIGHT—THE KILLING OF STEPHEN DAVIS AND WOUNDING OF ANGUS McLEAN.

On the morning of Oct. 4th, 1870, the entire band of outlaws visited the premises of Mr. Angus Leach, near Floral College. He hah a brandy still, and distilled for the neighborhood. From this fact it was afterwards known as the "Brandy Raid." After placing a guard over Mr. Leach, they proceeded to help themselves to anything they could find, and the brandy especially; of this they carried off a large quantity. On the same day the news of the affair reached Maxton, Capt. Murdock McLean gathered together seven or eight men and went in pursuit of the robbers by way of the Lumberton road on the other side of Lumber River from Mr. Leach's. This movement took the outlaws by surprise, as they did not expect any one to be after them on that side of the river. It was on this side of the river that George Applewhite lived, and the robbers called up at his house to have a "good time" over the captured brandy. About this time Capt. McLean, with his squad, arrived. The outlaws ran into an old pine field near by, and endeavored to conceal and protect themselves by getting the stumps and bushes between them and the militia. The firing now began in real earnest. During the fire Stephen Davis rusherd into the midst of the robbers, and Henry Berry shot him in the head, wounding him mortally. Mr. Davis did not fall, but reeled and staggered off into the river swamp near by, and was reported among the wounded and missing. Angus McLean swam the river and got to Mr. Gilbert's house, he being slightly wounded in the foot. This was, as I

before stated, October 4th, 1870.   Next morning, the 5th,
search was made for Mr. Davis, but he could not be
found, all who were engaged in the fight were sure that
Davis was wounded, as they saw him turn his head to
one side when fired upon by H. B. Lowrie.   A messenger was dispatched to Maxton, his place of business, to
ascertain if he had arrived, but found he had not.

Sheriff McMillan having received intelligence of this
affair, came to the Red Banks with five or six men, who
joined him on his way; he reached the Banks at 3
o'clock the morning after the fight.   Nothing could be
done towards searching for the wounded— perhaps dying—man before daylight.   All were satisfied that he
was killed, mortally wounded or captured by the outlaws.   He was found at 10 o'clock the day after the
fight, in the river swamp, lying on his face in the mud,
unconscious and nearly famished, not having drank
any water since the evening before.   He was taken to
the house of Mr. Roberts, where medical attention was
given him, but to no purpose; the fatal shot had pene-
trated the brain of the brave and gallant Davis—he
who had stood the storm of shot and shell on many a
battle-field, to be slain by the hands of a robber and
midnight assassin.   Mr. Davis was placed on the cars
and conveyed to Maxton, where all that kind friends
and physicians could do was done, but it was of no
avail; he could not be aroused from the lethargy into
which he had fallen, and he passed quietly away to the
spirit land.   A brave, daring man, in his death Robeson
county lost one of her best and most noble citizens.

THE MURDER OF MR. J. TAYLOR.

On the morning of the 8th of October, 1870, the dead body of one Malcomb Sanderson was found near the saw mill of Mr. William C. McNeill, of the county of Robeson.   An inquest was held over his body by Coroner Robert Chaffin, and the verdict was, "Deceased came to his death by gun-shot wounds from parties unknown."

Mr. McNeill's son-in-law, Mr. John Taylor, was living with him at the time, and had been persecuted by Andrew Strong and others of the Lowrie band for the reason that he would not aid them in their atrocious crimes.   He was the victim upon whom they determined to fix this murder.   They therefore set about arranging their plans, and by some means succeeded in fixing the crime upon Mr. Taylor.   A warrant was forthwith issued for his arrest, and he was brought before a Justice of the Peace, arraigned and tried for the murder of said Sanderson, and found guilty by said Justice of the Peace.   Mr. Taylor's friends (and he had many) were indignant at the idea of such an outrage, and immediately determined to have him released on a writ of habeas corpus.   The Sheriff, Roderick McMillan, carried him to Rockingham, in Richmond county (Court being in session at that place) before his Honor Judge Russell, who, upon investigating the case, released him upon Mr. Taylor's giving a bond for his personal appearance at the next term of court held for Robeson county in the sum of five hundred dollars, and Mr. Taylor returned to his distressed family.   His enemies not being satisfied in their efforts to deprive him of his liberty, set about the second time to annoy him.   One Mar-

tin Ransom sued out a peace warrant against him, and
he was re-arrested and arraigned before a magistrate
again, who bound him in a heavy bond to keep the
peace.   One of Mr. Taylor's friends endeavored to compromise the affair, but did not succeed in effecting anything, and Mr. Taylor must await his trial at the next
term of the court.   After refusing to comply with Mr.
Taylor's terms of compromise, Martin Ransom returned
home, and, it is supposed, held a conference with the
outlaws, who must have given him an inkling of their
intentions, for he retraced his steps to Lumberton and
withdrew the warrant.   Not exceeding three days there-
after, in going from his home to the depot at Moss Neck
Mr. Taylor received his death wounds from the hands
of Henry Berry Lowrie, Stephen Lowrie and Boss
Strong, who, from the side of the mill-dam, fired on him,
the entire load from one of their weapons passing through
his head, scattering his brains and sending them floating
on the waters of the pond.   Thus fell at the hands of
these fiends incarnate another of Robeson county's high-
toned, noble sons, leaving a young wife and one son to
mourn for him.   My pen almost fails to be guided to record the atrocious deed.   At the time Mr. Taylor was
killed there was a detachment of Battery A, 4th U. S.
Artillery, stationed within two hundred yards of the
spot where Mr. Taylor fell.   Right here a very natural
question arises, viz: Why this detachment allowed such
a crime to be perpetrated in broad open daylight, and
so near them?

Perhaps those soldiers can best answer, but we will
take the liberty, notwithstanding, of saying they were
well pleased, if not aiders and abettors in all the deep,
dark wrongs committed against the people of Robeson

county by that band of desperadoes that so long infested our country, making the hearts of her sons and daughters to throb with anguish, and weep tears that naught can ever dry.

JOHN SANDERS, THE DETECTIVE.

In the year A. D. 1869, in the month of November, John Sanders, a police officer from Boston, and a native of Nova Scotia, at the instance of some leading Conservatives in Robeson county, settled in Scuffletown, and commenced teaching the Indian children how to spell and read. To cover up and conceal his design he was accredited by the Sheriff of New Hanover county to some of the leading Republicans of the county. John Sanders' scheme of capturing the outlaws was a shrewd one. Aware that they were anxious to leave their old haunts and the swamps of Robeson, and get safely out of the States to Mexico or to the frontier, he proposed to show them the way, assume to be their protector and friend, and had prepared a wagon, and on the 19th of November, 1870, had the wagons packed with their families the outlaws having fully agreed to slip off with them under the cover of darkness, Sanders having arranged beforehand to have them intercepted at some designated point in Georgia. To bind the Scuffletonians to his confidence by extraordinary means, he pretended to organize Masonic lodges throughout Scuffletown whilst teaching school. He spent over twelve months in persevering cunning to win the skeptical hearts of the bandits, and in order to appease the white population, told the uninitiated that he was a veritable Ku Klux. He got

into several fisticuff fights with white men, about his
manner and mode of living, on account of his living
among the Scuffletonians and teaching school among
them.

Sanders was a large, portly man, of great muscular
power, possessing a kind, benignant look, a high, broad
forehead, winning manners, with much keenness of apprehension and undoubted boldness.   But he was betrayed, and there is reason to believe that his fate is to
be attributed to the want of due caution on the part of
some one who had learned his purposes.   He died as he
had lived in mystery and out of the reach or sight of
pitying man.   He was taken captive by H. B. Lowrie
and the other bandits on the morning of November 21st,
A. D. 1870, in a bay near the residence of W.C. McNeill,
and was never again seen by mortal eyes except by the
outlaws.   On the night previous to his capture H. B.
Lowrie and his associates had fifty-six of the Indians
of Scuffletown as accomplices, guarding the roads to
give the signal when Sanders would enter their lines,
and when poor Sanders entered their lines he heard the
rough word, "Halt!"   Almost immediately the voice of
Sanders was heard by some other white prisoners saying. "I surrender."   The outlaws then marched Sanders
off to a secret camp on the Back Swamp, called the
"Devil's Deer," (den) between Inman's bridge and the
Back Swamp, not far from the residence of Zach T.
McLaughlin, and proceeded forthwith with devilish
malignity to torture him by firing volleys over his head,
bruising him with gun-stocks and clubs, and finally by
administering doses of arsenic to him and opening his
veins with a pen-knife.   For three days, or until Thursday, these horrible wretches surrounded their white

victim, their dull blue eyes calmly enjoying his agonies, and he was reminded every hour that escape or mercy were hopeless, or at least out of the question.

The fortitude and philosophy of Sanders gained the respect of his murderers, and before carrying his sentence into execution they permitted him to write a farewell letter to his wife and family, which they posted by mail with a sort of grim and military observance of justice. Human or savage nature seldom presents a picture so atrocious as this of Sanders, guarded in the wild swamps of Carolina, but almost within the sound of Christian firesides, looking into inevitable and violent death after days of pain. The object of keeping Sanders alive so long has never been explained. Whether due to divided counsels or love of persecuting him while still alive, or the desire to wrest information from him, has been, and ever will remain, in doubt and shrouded in mystery. To die thus miserably in the swamps of Scuffletown, among the human moccasins that infested it, was indeed a miserable death. On Thursday night the outlaws told Sanders that his time had come, and they blindfolded his eyes and tied him to a tree. He made a few words of prayer and gave a signal, and Steve Lowrie, the meanest of the outlaws, emptied both barrels of his shot-gun into the body of the poor, helpless John Sanders.

The end of the unfortunate Sanders was related by Henderson Oxendine, one of the outlaws, prior to his execution, and was fully confirmed afterwards by Henry Berry Lowrie, who told several white men in the county that "they were compelled to kill Sanders in order to save themselves; that they all pitied him," &c. After the hanging of Henderson Oxendine, a party of twenty-five soldiers and citizens, led by Major Thomas and Lieutenants Howe and Simpson followed the directions given by Oxendine in his confession, and without difficulty, found the camp where Sanders had been confined. It was in the thickest part of Back Swamp, on an oak island, and scattered around were the spade and some cooking utensils. They proceeded to search for the remains, and found them decently wrapped in a blanket, with the hands folded in a dignified manner, and the daguerreotype of the murdered man's wife reverently placed upon his breast. The cool particularities and deliberation make the tragedy even more heinous by the awe which they inspired; it was murder with the appearance of sovereignty and martial right. No crime known to modern society presents such dark features as the killing of Sanders, and to this day the people of Robeson turn pale at the bloody reminiscence. This occurrence will frighten the rising generation of Carolina for the century to come. The remains of the unfortunate John Sanders were decently re-interred in a neat coffin by the Sheriff of the county.

Peace to his ashes !

KILLING OF ZACH McLAUGHLIN.

It being positively ascertained that McLaughlin belonged to the robber clan, and accompanied them in all their predatory visits in the neighborhood, the Sheriff, Roderick McMillan, summoned his posse and went to his house to arrest and carry him before a Justice of the Peace for trial. Zack not being aware that his complicity with the "gang" was known, generally remained at the house of his mother in the day, and at night-fall .

sallied forth to join his chosen comrades. The Sheriff had no difficulty in finding and arresting him. The premises were searched, but there was nothing found that could be identified; he, however, was carried to Red Banks, tried, and proven guilty of robbing the house of a Mr. Register in the neighborhood; although blacked at the time, he was recognized by a young lady visitor, who appeared as a witness against him at the time of trial. He was then taken to Lumberton and lodged in jail; he soon made his escape and entered the band in good earnest. He was recognized as one of the party who robbed the house of Mr. Zach. Fulmore. It becoming a certain fact that he really belonged to the band, he was outlawed by the proper authorities, and killed by Henry Biggs under the following circumstances : On the night of the 21st of December, 1870, Biggs met McLaughlin at the house of Mr. Noah Duncan. After supper he asked Biggs to walk out with him, which he did; after going some distance from the house, McLaughlin drew a pistol on Biggs and commenced cursing him, telling him that he had tried to persuade him long enough to join their band, and that he should compel him that night to go and aid him in robbing some cabins belonging to turpentine hands in the neighborhood. Biggs being unarmed, had no choice but to accompany him. The negroes were all sleeping soundly, and Zach. had no difficulty in appropriating to himself such articles as he thought proper. He left their cabins minus clothing, a watch, carpet-sack, boots, shoes, provisions, &c. He was drunk, and did not go far before he complained of being sleepy and very much fatigued; he ordered Biggs to kindle a fire, which he proceeded to do, followed up by Zack. with a drawn revolver in his

hand.   As soon as the fire was made, Zach. lay down
(making Biggs lie down with him) with his gun under his
head, and a belt around his waist with three large sized
pistols in it.   Soon he was snoring loudly.   Biggs concluded that the time was at hand to put an end to the
life of one of the villains of Robeson.   Reaching over
he gently withdrew a pistol from his belt, and putting
the muzzle to the back of the outlaw's head, fired, the
ball passing through and coming out near the eye.
Biggs leaped over the body and fired again, the ball
coming through near the ear.   Biggs took his arms and
concealed them in the woods, then reported to a Justice
of the Peace.   A party going out and identifying the
body, the reward of two hundred dollars offered by
the county was paid over to Biggs.

The reader will recollect that McLaughlin was the
murderer of Owen C. Norment in March preceding his
death.   He was considered by all who knew him as
more brutal than any of the gang.   He was the first to
meet his merited fate.

THE FATE OF HENDERSON OXENDINE.

On Saturday night, February 26th, 1871, the follow-
ing young men, John S. McNeill, Angus Archie McNeill,
William McNeill, John K. McNeill, Alexander McNeill,
Daniel McNeill, Hector McNeill, David McNeill, Archie
D. McCallum, W. Frierson Buie. Frank McKay, George
W. McKay, and Archibald Brown, captured Henderson
Oxendine in the house of his brother-in-law, George
Applewhite, and formally committed him to jail in Lum-
berton on Monday morning following, showing their
magnanimity in the act of committing him to jail, for he

was then an outlaw by the laws of his country.   A price
had been set on his head by the civil authorities on account of his many crimes, but these young men were as
generous as they were brave, and instead of killing him
outright, delivered him up to the civil authorities, and
insisted that he should be regularly tried by court and jury;
consequently, on Wednesday week following he was put
upon his trial in an open court in Lumberton, before his
Honor Daniel L. Russell, Jr., and after a fair and impar-
tial trial, found guilty of the crimes charged to him.
The Judge then sentenced him to be hanged on the 15th
of April, which sentence was carried into execution on
the day appointed inside the jail yard at Lumberton.

Thus passed away another of the Robeson county outlaws, in the 28th year of his age.   He was a thick-set,
but trim, Indian, with straight black hair, and rather an
indifferent face.   He made a full confession of his
crimes before his execution, and died almost stoically,
without a sigh.   Henderson Oxendine was the only outlaw that was hanged for being implicated in the murder of ex-Sheriff King.   Steve Lowrie and George Applewhite were also found guilty of being implicated in
that tragedy, but escaped out of jail before sentence
was passed on them.   John Dial, also another Indian,
outlawed for the same offense, turned State's evidence
and thus saved his neck although he was equally as guilty as the others.

BILLY McKOY

was an old colored man living on the plantation of Mr.
Sandy McKenzie.   He had incurred the wrath of the
robber clan and their friends, not only by standing aloof

from them, but also by casting his vote in every election
with the whites and avowing his principles to be con-
servative.   They commenced annoying the old man by
stealing his chickens, vegetables, &c.   They came to his
houe early in the spring of 1871, and told him that they
heard his house was the headquarters of the colored
soldiers.   He told them it was not so; they had spent
one night there only; that he was from home when they
came, and on returning at night, found them snugly
quartered beneath his roof; that he had no authority
to order them out, and therefore submitted quietly to
their company.   The robbers then said, "You vote with
white men."   He replied, "Yes; I have a right to vote
as I please, and that is my choice."   They accused him
of telling falsehoods to Mr. J. M. McNair about them.
This he denied.   Old Billy was badly frightened, and
to set him somewhat at ease, they told him that they
would not kill him, but intended giving him a good
whipping.   A voice in the dark said, "No, don't whip
the old man."   Boss Strong said, "Yes, and we will
take his clothes off to do it."   H. B. Lowrie ordered
him whipped with his clothes on, which Boss did, whipping him severely.   He knew four of the crowd to be
Steve and H. B. Lowrie and the two Strongs; the other
three he did not recognize.   He had a near neighbor, a
negro, working on the same plantation, by the name of
Ben Bethea, who was an avowed enemy of Old Billy,
and who also belonged to the robber clan.   He was in-
strumental in having the old fellow whipped.   Some
time during the following winter, this Bethea was taken
from his house by a company of armed men and carried about three miles off and shot.   He justly deserved

the punishment meted out to him. Not only a co-worker
with the clan, but if any one gave him the slightest cause
for offence, sought revenge either on their persons or
property by carrying malicious tales to his confederates
in crime, thus setting them on to do harm to the offender. He was a native of South Carolina, and was an
accomplice in the robbing and burning of the house of
a widow lady in that State soon after the surrender.
The authorities attempted to capture him, and he sought
refuge in Robeson county, joining the robber band,
where he was finally overtaken, and a just punishment
for his crimes awarded him.

AN AGREEMENT OR COMPACT OF ELEVEN YOUNG MEN IN ROBESON COUNTY.

In March, 1871, a plan formed for ridding and free-
ing entirely Robeson county of the Lowrie outlaws was
entered into by F. M. Wishart, Mudoch A. McLean,
George L. McKay, Frank McKay, John A. McKay, W.
H. McCallum, J. Douglas McCallum, Archie D. McCallum, Archie J. McFadyen, Malcom McNeill, (Greeley)
and Faulk J. Floyd, and persistently carried out. Arm-
ing themselves with navy revolvers, Spencer, Henry and
Winchester guns, they immediately entered on the campaign, and went forth to hunt the outlaws in their
swampy retreats and fastnesses in Scuffletown, determined to kill or be killed—determined to vindicate the
name and fame of their native county. These brave
spirits under all the discouraging circumstances which
surrounded them, stood the stalwart braves of our county, like Warsaw's last champion.

"Oh heavens! they said, Our bleeding Country save,
   Is there no hand on high to shield the brave?
What though destruction sweeps these lovely plains,
   Rise, fellow-men! Our country yet remains;
By that dread name, we wave the sword on high,
   And swear for her to live, for her to die".

This was a "dark and doleful period" in the history
of Robeson county.   Some of our best citizens had been
forced to leave the county simply because they had taken a part in ferreting out these outlaws.   Our young
men and old men had been branded abroad as a set of
cowards; we had become a bye-word and a reproach
among our sister counties; we had been considered by
the outer world as colleagues with them in their murders, arsons, treason and rebellion.   No people in any
country have been so abused and villified as the citizens
of Robeson county, simply because they did not rise up
and extirpate the Lowrie gang.   Few men would have
essayed to do what these noble, heroic men attempted;
few men would have gone forth voluntarily as they did
and encountered the perils to which they were exposed
by day and by night; often were they wearied, often
did they suffer from hunger, from thirst, from weary
limbs, aching heads, wet clothes, cold, frost, heat; yet
on they went tramp, tramp, through midnight darkness,
through rain, sunshine, through the almost impenetrable bays and swamps of Scuffletown, encountering the
frowns of the Indian, the hisses of the negro race, and
sometimes the scowls of a few of the white race who
had black hearts; often they were ridiculed, slurred and
censured, yet they braved all with courage and fortitude without being moved.   On the 8th of April they
saw at a distance the whole of the outlaw gang, who,

on perceiving them, made off precipitately into the low
grounds of Lumber River. On the following Saturday
night these brave and intrepid men met again at Plain-
view. Owing to sickness and other causes only five of
them reported, viz: George L. McKay, Franklin Mc-
Kay, W. H. McCallum, Archie D. McCallum and J.
Douglas McCallum; after consultation they determined,
however, to go to the house of the notorious outlaw,
George Applewhite, dark as the night was, and wait the
dawn of day, which was to be the Sabbath. Stationing
themselves near his residence, on a path leading across
the Juniper in the direction of the Carolina Central Railway, they remained there until 4 o'clock p. m., when, to
their surprise, they saw George Applewhite proceeding directly towards them(all was confusion for a few moments),
when W. H. McCallum fired upon him from a distance not
more than twenty paces, the load taking effect in the neck
of the outlaw; he returned the fire simultaneously, turning his back, however. Frank McKay fired on him,
his load taking effect in his back. George L. McKay
and J. Douglas McCallum, hearing the clash of arms,
rose up and also fired on him when near the edge of the
swamp. Here he reeled and fell. Fearing that the entire outlaw gang was near at hand, these young men left
the blood-stained spot, not, however, before they picked
up a sack containing a hat and a pair of shoes, dropped
by the outlaw, also the hat he had on when shot. Sending a messenger to Lumberton after the Sheriff in order
to deliver the body of the outlaw to him, they separated
for the night. Returning in the morning with the Sheriff
and some other gentlemen, the body of George Apple-

white could nowhere be found, the other outlaws having removed him during the night.

He was not killed, as was subsequently learned, but was seriously wounded, and was kept concealed until his wounds healed so that he could travel, when he slipped away from the county, not even his comrades, the outlaws knowing, his intention.   But he made good his escape.   Subsisting on fruit and watermelons until beyond Fayetteville, where he was less afraid of being recognized, he began to ask for work and food.   Finally he reached Goldsboro, where he remained for several months—when his whereabouts was discovered.   He was again arrested and placed in Whiteville jail, was tried and acquitted under the "Amnesty Act."   Thus was the gallows cheated, and he whose hand was stained with the blood of the good and honorable and aged citizens of our country, given life and liberty.   Alas! for justice.

It will be remembered that George Applewhite was outlawed for killing ex-Sheriff King, for which crime he was twice tried and condemned to be hanged, but his counsel taking an appeal to the Supreme Court, he escaped from jail and returned to his former haunts and depredation, where he was wounded; and from whence he escaped to Goldsboro.

After the wounding of George Applewhite by these young men the bandts became more wary.   The hunt for them, however, was still kept up by Geo. L. McKay, Frank McKay, J. D. McCallum, A. D. McCallum, F. M. Wishart, M. McNeill, Archie McFadyen and F. J. Floyd, assisted occasionally by Rod. McMillan and A. M. McLean.   From sheer fatigue they became exhausted, and on the last day of June they came out of Scuffletown, and the County Commissioners called out ten men in each Township to serve one week by turns, and placed the same men under command of F. M. Wishart, mith headquarters at Buie's Store in the heart of Scuffletown.

F. M. Wishart entered on the duty assigned him on the 8th of July following, and kept up the pursuit of the outlaws unremittedly. On the 10th of July several persons suspected of harboring and sympathizing with the outlaws were arrested by order of the Sheriff, including the wives of H. B. Lowrie, George Applewhite and Andrew Strong. The party who arrested the wives of the outlaws were fired on from an ambuscade by the outlaws when near Buie's Store, immediately on the railway, and Archibald A. McMillan was instantly killed, and Archibald Brown and Hector McNeill were mortally wounded, from the effects of which they died next morning. Berry Barnes and Alex. Brown were also slightly wounded. Notwithstanding these casualties the other four men returned the fire and caused the outlaws to retreat to the woods. They carried the prisoners in triumph and delivered them to Col. F. M. Wishart. On the same evening the outlaws engaged a company of men under Capt. Charles McRae, at a point on Lumber River known as "Wire-Grass Landing," about 5 o'clock p. m.

THE FIGHT AT WIRE GRASS LANDING.

On the morning of the 10th of July, 1871, a company of the militia called out by the Sheriff, consisting of fourteen men from Alfordsville and Thompson townships, reported to Capt. Wishart for duty at Buie's Store. They were ordered to go to the house of Andrew Strong

and arrest his wife and carry her to a point on the road
leading from Harper's Ferry to Red Banks Bridge,
where they were to meet a party that had been sent to
arrest the wives of Henry B. Lowrie and others of the
outlaws. They arrested Andrew Strong's wife and
proceeded with her to the point designated, where they
waited several hours for the party that was to convey
her to headquarters, which, through a misunderstanding,
had gone another way. During the afternoon, as the
party did not arrive, the Captain detailed four men
from the company to escort her to said destination.
The ten men that were left then proceeded to Wire
Grass Landing, on Lumber River, below Harper's Ferry Bridge. A short time after they reached this place
they heard talking near by, and soon discovered that it
was a party in a boat on the river, and they were coming towards them. When they reached a point about
seventy-five yards above the landing, they stopped.
They heard them wading in the water, and knew that
some of the party had left the boat. After remaining
very quiet for some time, the canoe again started down
the river, which, on making a short bend, was clearly in
view. H. B. Lowrie was the only occupant of the
boat, and as he was greeted by a volley from the guns
of the militia, he sprang into the water, keeping the canoe
between him and the enemy as a kind of portable
breast-work. His firing was harmless, as was much
from the random shooting of those in the bushes. (Those
of the party that had gotten out of the boat were concealed in the bushes). There were four mulattoes with
the militia; on opening fire they ran, but when ordered
back obeyed and behaved very quietly throughout the
fight. The post was held by the militia until their am-

munition was exhausted and the command given to retire. In this fight Mr. Duncan McCormick and Charles Smith were wounded, though not seriously. The damage done to the outlaws could not be ascertained.

On the 14th of July following the Lowrie bandits went to the residence of Mr. John McNair and behaved very insultingly, although Mr. McNair, previous to this feud, had often treated them very kindly, frequently selling them corn and meat on a credit and waiting patiently for his pay. On this day, however, they ordered Mr. McNair to write the following note:

Mr. James Sinclair : If our wives are not released and sent home by next Monday morning there will be worse times in Robeson county than there ever has been yet. We will commence and drench the county in blood and ashes.

<blockquote>
Signed   {   H. B. LOWRIE,
           STEVE LOWRIE,
           ANDREW STRONG.
</blockquote>

They then ordered Mr. McNair to hitch his horse to his buggy and proceed with it to Lumberton and deliver it to James Sinclair, which Mr. McNair did, leaving no white person on the place except his wife (Mrs. McNair). Arriving at Lumberton about 10 o'clock a. m., Mr. Mc-Nair delivered the note to James Sinclair, who, after reading it, directed him to hand it to the Sheriff, which he did, and after the Sheriff read it, he told Mr. McNair to inform the outlaws that the people of Robeson county were not to be tampered with in that way, and driven by mere threats into measures by these outlaws, and the white men of Robeson in all time to come branded as cowards. Mr. McNair returned and met the outlaws about three miles below his residence, on the road to Lumber-

ton, and delivered the message of the Sheriff to them,
which they received with a dark, ominous scowl, but
offered no violence to Mr. McNair.

On Monday following, quite a number of the old grey-
headed citizens of Robeson county went to Lumberton
and held a consultation with the Sheriff and County
Commissioners, and the conclusion arrived at was, that
taking all things into consideration, it was probably best
to release the wives of the outlaws and send them home,
inasmuch as they (the wives) were not responsible for the
acts of their husbands, and also because it was believed
at the time that their release would have a good effect
on the rest of the Indian race.   They were therefore
released and sent home next day.

The next week following, Adjutant-General Gorman
appeared on the scene of action with part of a company
of Federal soldiers, asking the county of Robeson for an
equal number of volunteers to co-operate with him in
capturing the outlaws, when the following named gen-
tlemen responded to the call: F. M. Wishart, Colonel;
James Nicholson McLean, Captain; J. C. McKellar, First
Lieutenant; James McBryde, Second Lieutenant; John
S. McNeill, Third Lieutenant; and the following privates:
Henry McCallum, J. T. McCormic, A. A. McGirt, C. Mc-
Rae, E. C. McNeill, Gilchrist McGirt, Daniel McKenzie,
James McQueen, Archie McDonald, James McGoogan,
Alexander McGirt, Malcom McNeill (Greely), Samuel
Barnes, John Cobb, Henry Biggs, Frank Currie, Joseph
Phillips, Archie Johnson, Duncan Campbell, Daniel
Campbell, Thomas Purcell, W. C. Smith.

These men remained with Adjutant-General Gorman
in Scuffletown two months, and were disbanded without
capturing a single outlaw, simply because the outlaws

evaded them on all occasions. The volunteers generally, and the true men of Robeson county believed at
the time, and believe to this day, that the Adjutant-General of the State was in collusion with the outlaws, as
was every negro in the county. Thus terminated this
campaign of Adjutant-General Gorman, without accom-
plishing anything; in the mean time, however, the predatory warfare on the part of the outlaws went on without any cessation, robbing whom they pleased and when
they pleased, depleting the whole country around Scuffletown of guns and pistols, and whatever else they saw
fit to take; turning the heads of the Indians and prompt-
ing negro imitators; and training up the very children
of Scuffletown to be barbarians, with the lust for plunder and rapine. Indeed, after the failure of Gen. Gorman to capture them, the outlaws showed more desper-
ation than ever; they seemed to fear nothing, whilst
they showed a ferocity, premeditation and insolence
frightful to behold; spreading terror and dismay wher-
ever they saw fit to go; no one not an inhabitant of the
county at the time can realize the situation; nearly all
of our citizens, with here and there an honorable exception, seemed terror-stricken and dumb with dismay, for
they did not know at what hour the Lowrie bandits
would pounce down on them like an eagle on his prey,
and murder some male member of the family for some
imaginary wrong, or take away from them their hard
earnings.

Here we will relate an incident that occurred "not a
hundred miles" from Ashpole Presbyterian church to
J. C. McKellar and the squad of men under him (some
twelve in number): Lieutenant J. C. McKellar and his
men met on the road a well-to-do farmer and informed

him that he and his squad were going to his house for
their dinner; this well-to-do farmer told Mr. McKellar
and his men to go directly to his kitchen and order his
cook, a negress, to prepare dinner for them, so that it
might be told to the outlaws that he was forced to feed
the men that were hunting them. J. C. McKellar and
his men were incensed at the conduct of this well-to-do
farmer, but concluded, in order to retaliate on him, to
do as he had directed. So they went and ordered this
man's cook to fix up dinner for them, which, after being
fixed up, they ate with a gusto, and even to this day
when this circumstance is referred to, the men who partook of that dinner will laugh about the cowardice of
this well-to-do farmer, and say: "Well, he won't do to
tie to in a storm".

THE KILLING OF GILES INMAN.

On the 21st of April, 1871, the Sheriff of the county,
viz: Rod. McMillan, in connection with F. M. Wishart,
Archie D. McCallum, J. Douglas McCallum, Franklin
McKay, George L. McKay, Archie McFadyen and Malcom McNeill, surrounded H. B. Lowrie's house, when,
to their surprise, it was ascertained that the whole outlaw band were within. After consultation, it was
deemed prudent and wise that the Sheriff and Frank
McKay should go and hunt up recruits to capture the
whole outlaw gang. The Sheriff and Mr. McKay immediately set out on their errand, and coming to the
house of Mr. Hugh Inman, on Lumber River, about
three miles from H. B. Lowrie's, his two sons, Robert
and Giles Inman, went back with Mr. McKay to the assistance of the men left at H. B. Lowrie's house. In the

meantime, H. B. Lowrie and the other outlaws made
their escape through a "trap door and a tunnel", dug
some distance from the house of H. B. Lowrie, as was
afterwards ascertained; and they (the outlaws) throwing themselves back on the road which they supposed
would be traveled by the Sheriff on his return, ambus-
caded the recruits as they were crossing the Back Swamp
and fired on them, killing instantly Mr. Giles Inman, a
youth aged eighteen years, and wounded Mr. Frank
McKay.   Mr. McKay returned the fire.   Thus fell
another victim of their relentless fury and vindictive-
ness.   Mr. Inman was a resolute youth, and was anxious to apprehend these lawless marauders.   His father,
Mr. Hugh Inman, was a Republican in politics.   Some
time after this occurrence. H. B. Lowrie informed Mr.
Inman that he was sorry that he had killed his son Giles
(and well he might be); but this was only adding insult
to injury.   It was the sorrow which the lion has for the
lamb when in his power.

THE MURDER OF MURDOCH A. McLEAN AND HIS BROTHER HUGH McLEAN—ALSO THE WOUNDING OF ARCHIE D. McCALLUM.

The murder of the two brothers, Murdoch A. McLean
and Hugh McLean, was committed on the morning of
July 17th, 1871, on the public road, one mile south of
Maxton, on the Carolina Central Railway, near a mill
on Black Branch, in full view of the residence of Mrs.
Margaret McLean.   This feat was achieved after long
and cool deliberation on the part of the outlaws.   They
had often essayed to kill Murdoch A. McLean, and had
as often failed in their purpose.   Several times they had

waylaid him; several times they had lurked about the
premises of his mother in the darkness of the night, but
all to no purpose. Early on the morning of the 17th
Hugh McLean carried his sister to the residence of Mr.
M. C. McNair in an open buggy.   On his return home,
Murdoch A. McLean and Archie D. McCallum jumped
up into the buggy with Hugh and started off for Maxton
to hunt the robber band.   As the trio rode along about
three hundred yards from the residence of Mrs. Margaret
McLean they heard the rough word. "halt!"   Almost
instantly a gun was snapped at close quarters, from behind a "blind," by Henry Berry Lowrie.   Murdoch A.
McLean reached for his arms, but before he could bring
his gun to bear, he was riddled with buck-shot, and his
brother Hugh mortally wounded, the horse in the buggy
galloping off with the lifeless remains of the two brothers.
In the killing of Murdoch A. McLean, Henry Berry
Lowrie shed the blood of one of the noblest youthful
spirits in our country; indeed, he was a superb specimen
of the "Bonnie Scotch."

> "None knew him but to love him,
>   None named him but to praise."

He was in his thirty-first year of age when he fell,
honored, esteemed and loved by all who knew him for
the many noble traits of character.   Peace to his ashes !
But what shall we pen in regard to innocent Hugh
McLean, who was also killed at the same time?   Alas!
my pen falters—my hand trembles, when I recall this
double murder!   Innocent Hugh was in the twentieth
year of his age, and bid fair to become as noble and
generous a man as his brother Murdoch had been.
Archie D. McCallum, who was riding in the buggy
with the two brothers, sprang out on the ground, and in

doing so, his pistol fell out of its case; he, however, had
the coolness to stoop down and pick it up, and then to
run, for he saw the whole outlaw gang were at hand,
and knew if he remained that they would murder him
also.   He had not proceeded far when he was fired on
and wounded in his leg, but he made good his escape to
Maxton, although pursued by two of the gang to within
a few hundred yards of the depot.   When the news of
the occurrence spread abroad, the wildest consternation
seemed to seize many of the good citizens of Robeson
county.   All was confusion.   What to do next was the
main question.

COL. FRANK M. WISHART.

High on the "roll of honor" in the county of Robeson
stands the name of Col. Frank M. Wishart—a man that
would be noticed in any crowd on account of his showy
appearance.   He was an old Confederate officer, and
served throughout the war between the States   with
credit to himself and honor to his native county.   He was
a Republican in politics, and the only Republican in the
county of Robeson of any distinction who could or did
rise superior to party politics and take the side of bleeding, suffering humanity.   He possessed true nobleness of
mind and a lofty magnanimity of character, and through
"evil report as well as good," he bore himself with dig-
nity and disinterestedness, fearless of danger to his person or reputation.   All honor to Frank M. Wishart for
his noble example—all honor to his name for his exalted
patriotism.   True to his natural instincts, he joined the
compact of those eleven self-sacrificng men who determined to rid Robeson county of the Lowrie outlaws or

die in the attempt. He entered this compact early in
February, in the year 1871, and worked assiduously for
the capture of the outlaws until he fell a victim to their
treachery on the 16th day of May, A. D. 1872, in the
——year of his age. He met his sad and melancholy
fate on the main road leading from Lumberton to Rockingham, in Richmond county, about one and a half miles
from Lebanon Presbyterian Church, on the south side
of Lumber River, and about two miles from Red Banks
bridge, whither he had gone alone to have an interview
with the oulaws, in accordance with an agreement made
with them at Moss Neck on the previous Friday, as the
following particulars will delineate, taken from the Robe-
sonian (newspaper) on May 23rd, 1872:

"We are enabled to present some interesting particulars of the interview of Col. F. M. Wishart with the
outlaws at Moss Neck, a few days before his assassina-
tion by them. On Friday before his death, Col. Wishart was aboard the regular through freight train, which
arrived at Moss Neck at 3 o'clock p. m., and was at that
time occupying a seat in the conductor's cab in rear of
the train. Soon after the train halted, the two outlaws,
Andrew Strong and Stephen Lowrie, approached the
car and recognized Col. Wishart, and accosted him in a
civil and friendly way.   Stephen Lowrie inquired
whether he had any arms, and went aboard the cab to
satisfy himself on that point, Andrew Strong remaining
on the piazza of the store, within a few feet of the train.
Andrew was in his shirt-sleeves and wore only one pistol
in his belt, but Stephen carrie in his hand a Spencer rifle
and in his belt five elegant pistols—two Derringers, one
Smith & Wesson and two Colt's. On entering the car, Stephen demanded to see his arms, when Col. Wishart drew

aside the skirt of his coat and displayed the handle of a
repeater, which he assured the outlaw was the only
weapon he carried. Stephen at once made a grab at
the pistol, as if to snatch it from its place, but Col. Wishart foiled this attempt by dexterously leaping from the
car to the piazza of the store, where the other outlaw
was standing, and, confronting Stephen, who was standing in the door of the car from which he had just escaped, stood with his hand upon his pistol. Stephen and
Andrew both now assured him that they meant him no
harm. and only wished a friendly conference, and at
Andrew's request, he walked with him behind the store,
where they remained for sometime in conversation,
while Stephen remained on board the car, and seemed
to take no interest in what was passing between his comrade and Col. Wishart. As the train was about to move
off, Col. Wishart returned to the car, and meeting
Stephen on the platform, the latter was heard to say:
'When I send for, you come. I'll send a friend for you
in a few days, and you come and meet us,' and Col.
Wishart promised to do so.

The rest of this strange, sad story with its melancholy,
tragic end, is but too well known. On Thursday morning next, after this interview, a messenger—who it was
nobody knows, or ever will know, bore to Col. Wishart,
at Maxton, the summons which led him away to his
death. True to his word, he prepared to obey, and
saddling his mule, he rode directly, unarmed and alone,
to the spot named by the messenger. What occurred
was witnessed by no human eye besides those of the actors in the fearful tragedy; but in the afternoon of the
same day, a citizen of the neighborhood was horrified by
the discovery of the body of the gallant Wishart, all

stark and stiff and covered with gore, lying by the road-side. Two hideous, gaping wounds, one through the body and the other through the head, showed how foully he had been murdered. The mule on which he rode stood fastened to a limb near by, and appearances showed that when shot he was reclining on the earth whittling the end of a small stick and unsuspecting of danger. It is probable that these treacherous and cowardly fiends had concealed themselves in ambush near the spot, and the first intimation he had of their presence were the two shots that hurled his brave, unsuspecting soul into eternity.

JAMES McQUEEN, ALIAS DONAHOE.

Of all the men that have essayed to exterminate the Robeson outlaws, none have been more persevering than James McQueen, or Donahoe, as he is sometimes called. Slim and slender in form, peculiar and eccentric in manners, so much so that persons unacquainted with him look upon him at times as somewhat wild and romantic, quick in movement, showing agility and determination in every motion, about six feet high, with a small piercing gray eye, without much expression of countenance, he is the very personification of a gawky Scotchman, in his twenty-fifth year of age, a native of Richmond county, N. C. After reaching maturity, or becoming twenty-one years old, he left Mr. Donahoe in Richmond county, the gentleman who raised him, and after working a while in South Carolina, for wages, he purchased first a double-barreled shot gun and ammunition, and wended his way to Robeson county, going from house to house and telling the people that he wished to buy a tract of

land, and would sometimes examine tracts that were offered for sale, and then decline purchasing on the ground
that the price was too high; sometimes, too, he would offer to lease from some farmer a one-horse farm, &c.   In
this way he became acquainted with the people of Robeson and found out all about the Lowrie outlaws, and
who were their friends and who were their enemies—
in this way, too, he found out who were the true men of
the county, who would do to trust or confide in and not
betray him—he found out also the roads and by-paths
of Scuffletown—he sometimes would go with one company that were hunting the outlaws in Scuffletown, and
sometimes with another—his comrades, however, invariably found him reliable, always at his post, never
sleepy or drowsy, very particular where he went, and
when and how.   At last he took to going into Scuffletown
solitary and alone in the dead hours of the night along
by-paths and on roads that were not much traveled,
and when he arrived at the place where he wished to
watch for the passing of the outlaws, he would ensconce
himself in some thick undegrowth and remain as quiet as
a cat, watching for his prey to come along.   In this way
he became acquainted with the personal appearance of
the outlaws, their arms and accoutrements.   After pursuing the above course for some months, he furnished
himself with a Henry rifle, and had provisions cooked
up to last him three days, and wended his way to the
dreary swamps of Scuffletown on the 6th day of March,
A. D. 1872, and on the night following he arrived at the
house of Andrew Strong, on the south side of Lumber
river, about one mile from Harper's Ferry, and about
ten miles from Maxton, on the Carolina Central Rail-

way, and now we will permit him to tell his own statement of the facts in the case of killing Boss Strong:

JAMES McQUEEN'S, OR DONAHOES' VERSION OF THE KILL-
ING OF BOSS STRONG.

Last Thursday night, March 7th, I reached the house
of Andrew Strong, on the edge of Scuffletown, about
ten miles from Maxton, at 12 o'clock; I fixed a good
blind about a hundred and fifty yards from the house,
and lying down I watched the rest of the night and all
of the next day, eating some provisions I had brought
along.   About half-past seven p. m., Friday, Andrew
Strong came out of the woods, and after stopping and
looking around him in all directions, he went into the
house and directly came out and gave a low call, when
Boss Strong came out of the woods to the house; they
were each armed with two rifles and two or three revolvers.   A little after 8 o'clock, when I thought they
would be at supper, I slipped up to the house and looked in through the cat hole in the door, as I supposed
they were eating their supper by the light on the hearth.
A Miss Cummings was there, besides Flora, Andrew's
wife.   I kept watching, until Boss laid down on the
floor with his feet to the fire and his head towards me,
and commenced playing on a mouth harp; then I saw
my chance, and I pushed my rifle (a Henry) through the
cat-hole until it was not over three feet from his head,
and took a steady aim by the light and shot; when I
fired the women screamed and said "he's shot!" "no, he
isn't!" "yes, he is!" and I looked in as quick as I could
get my gun away.   Boss' arms and legs had fallen
straight from his body, and there was a little movement

of the shoulders, as if he was trying to get up.   Andrew
Strong was then standing in the shadow of the chimney
corner, and he stayed there until I left.   He said to his
wife, "Honey, you go out and see what it was," and
opened the door opposite the one I was at and pushed
her out, but she did not come around to the side where
I was, but went in directly and said there was nobody
about.   He sent her out again, telling her to look in the
corners and jams; but before she got well out, he said,
"Come back honey, he was blowing on that thing and
it busted and blowed his head off," and directly after he
said, "My God, he's shot in the head, and it must have
come from the cat-hole," and sent his wife out again;
then I slipped off.   When I returned the cat-hole was
shut up and the house was all dark.   I then came back to
Maxton, made up a party and went back to the house of
Andrew Strong; arriving there about 10 o'clock a. m.
on Saturday, we found Rhoda Lowrie, wife of Henry
B. Lowrie and sister to Boss and Andrew Strong, wiping
up the blood on the floor that had issued from the wound
inflicted on Boss Strong.   There were several women
present, but the body of Boss Strong was nowhere to be
found; upon inquiry, we ascertained from the women
present, that Steve Lowrie and Andrew Strong had just
removed the remains of Boss Strong to some secluded
spot, and had threatened the women present, that if
they watched them, in order to see which way they
went, that they would come back and killthem.   So
I, and the party that accompanied me, returned to
Maxton the same evening, without finding the body of
Boss Strong.

The illustration on page 129 is the house where Boss Strong was
killed.   He was the trusted comrade of Henry Berry Lowrie.

The above closes James McQueen's statement in regard the killing of the outlaw, Boss Strong. Subsequently it leaked out through the women present that Boss
Strong was shot through the head, and died almost instantly, and on the oath of these same women, the Legislature of North Carolina, at its session of 1873-'74,
passed a bill authorizing the State Treasurer to pay to
James McQueen $5,000 for killing Boss Strong.

Boss Strong was the youngest of the gang of the outlaws, and was the most trusted and inseperable companion of Henry Berry Lowrie, his brother-in-law. He was
only in his twentieth year when killed. He was nearly
white, with dark, short-cut hair that had somewhat of a
reddish tinge, slightly curling. A thick down appeard
on his lips, but otherwise he was beardless. He had
that dull, bluish eye belonging to all Scuffletonians generally, and was generally silent and taciturn, but he had
the demon in him, and when aroused, he had a dogged,
determined lock. He had the courage of a bull-pup,
and next to Henry Berry Lowrie, the leader, was re-
garded as the worst of the party. His hands were dyed
deep in the blood of both old and young. He was about
five feet ten inches high, thick set, with a full face and
would weigh one hundred and sixty-five pounds. Like
his leader, he generally killed at close quarters, seldom at
more than five to ten yards. He met up with his match
though, when James McQueen fired at him through the
cat-hole with his Henry rifle. After James McQueen
killed Boss Strong, the other outlaws became very shy
and were seldom seen, or heard of, for several months.
James McQueen, however, still kept up the hunt for
them, and never desisted entirely until the last outlaw
was killed. The outlaws dreaded James McQueen more

than any other man that ever took the field against
them, and well they might fear him, for he moved about
almost as noiselessly as a cat,

THE WISHART COMPANY IN 1872.

After the Lowrie outlaws had decoyed and slain in
cold blood the noble, and patriotic Col. F. M. Wishart,
they sent a message to his two brothers, viz: A Strong
Wishart and Robert E. Wishart on the 15th of July,
1872, to leave the county, or they might expect to be
killed. Instead of obeying the orders of the outlaws, they
armed themselves with Spencer rifles, and getting Mr.
James McKay and James Campbell to join them, they
set out on the 17th of July for the dreary swamps of
Scuffletown, to hunt the outlaws.   On the 18th of July
they were reliably informed that Tom Lowrie, one of the
outlaws, was in the habit of visiting regularly, the house
of one Furney Prevatt.   They immediately wended
their way thither, and arriving there after nightfall,
secreted themselves in the woods as near as possible
without discovery.   Remaining there that night and the
whole of the next day until after dark, they ventured up
nearer to the house in order to watch the movements
inside.   They soon discovered Tom Lowrie come out
of the house accompanied by a woman and go into a
crib near by.   They also perceived that they could not
kill the outlaw without endangering the life of the
woman; so while waiting outside, they heard Tom L. say
that he intended to go next day to Union Chapel, to a
public speaking that was to come off there.   They then
withdrew to the woods and concluded that they would

endeavor to intercept the outlaw on his way to Union
Chapel. Taking with them a guide, they halted at a
point where the main road crosses the Holly Swamp.
Here they stationed themselves, awaiting the dawn of
the morning of July 20th. Lying in great suspense and
anxiety, until about 8 o'clock a. m., they heard voices
approaching them in the direction of the Prevatt house.
Sure enough, Tom Lowrie and Furney Prevatt soon
made their appearance. Coming to the place on the
road where the Wishart company crossed, the outlaw
stopped to examine the footprints and Furney Prevatt
walked on. After looking at the footprints of A. S.
Wishart and associates, the outlaw was heard to say
that he "Would go to Union Chapel that day or die in
the attempt." These were the last words ever uttered
by Tom Lowrie, the outlaw, for just then Mr. James
McKay fired on him. Turning to run, Mr. A. S. Wishart fired on him also, with a Spencer rifle, the ball passing clear through his body. The outlaw, however, ran
some fifty yards and fell with a heavy groan. Mr. A.
S. Wishart procuring the assistance of Mr. David Davis,
and pressing a wagon that was passing at the time, removed the body of the dead outlaw out of the swamp,
taking off of his person three pistols, a Spencer rifle, a gold
watch, which belonged to Mr. John McNair, one hundred
and thirty dollars in currency and a Spanish dollar.
The company placed the body in a wagon and proceeded with it to Lumberton, and formally delivered it to the
Sheriff of the county, who paid them two hundred dollars, the amount of the reward offered for his body,
dead or alive, by the County Commissioners, placing
also in their hands the necessary papers to draw
six thousand dollars out of the State Treasury, the

amount offered for his apprehension by the State authorities, which was promptly paid by the Treasurer of
the State, and equally divided between A. S. Wishart,
R. E. Wishart, James McKay, James Campbell and
David Davis.

Thus passed away another of the Lowrie bandits,
whose back had been peppered once before by Frank
McKay, Archie D. McCallum, J. Douglas McCallum and
others, but got off with a bloody shirt sticking to his
back. Tom Lowrie was thirty-seven years of age when
killed; possessed broad shoulders; a strong and active
body; straight black hair; would weigh about 180 lbs.,
and was five feet ten inches high. A thieving sneak he
was, capable of murder or anything else mean. He had
a bluish gray eye, and when observed closely, a furtive
look that seemed to take in the whole situation at a
glance. He had been twice captured and placed in jail,
each time making his escape; but this time he went to
"that bourne from whence no traveler returns."

After Tom Lowrie was killed, the "Wishart" company did not cease in their exertions to kill the remaining outlaws. They remained in Scuffletown all the
time, watching the movements of the outlaws. The only member that left the company was Mr. James Campbell, and he left it on account of his health. Mr. Frank
Floyd took his place and remained one month. Mr.
Alf. Prevatt took Mr. Floyd's place and remained eight
months. Mr. James McQueen staid also with the company three weeks; the remainder of his time in Scuffletown he was alone. Mr. A. C. Bridgers was also a
member of the company for several months in 1872.
On the 10th of August A, McE. McCallum joined the
Wishart company, word having been sent him to leave

the county by the outlaws, because he had given the
Wishart company something to eat; instead of leaving,
he joined the company that was hunting them. Mr.
McCallum remained with the company until the 10th of
December, and on the 17th went to the State of Georgia
to please his father and friends. Staying there seven
months he returned to Robeson and rejoined the same
company. He found the company then composed of A. S.
Wishart, R. E. Wishart, James McKay, Ernest Lemon,
Buck Hilliard and a negro by the name of Solomon Morrison, (the only negro, be it said to his credit, that ever
voluntarily hunted the outlaws). The hunt for the re-
maing outlaw, viz: Steve Lowrie, was still kept up by
this company. Two members of the outlaw band had
been previously killed viz : Boss Strong by James Mc-
Queen, and Andrew Strong, by William Wilson, so that
Steve Lowrie was the only outlaw that roamed at large,
and he became so shy that it was a difficult matter to
see or hear of his whereabouts. However, James Mc-
Kay, Ernest Lemon and the negro Solomon Morrison
shot at him a short time before he was killed while conversing with Nat Clark, near Clark's residence, but they
were too far off to hurt the outlaw. These same men,
together with A. McE. McCallum, were stationed on the
main road not more than half of a mile distant from the
place where Steve Lowrie was killed, on the night preceding his killing, waiting for Steve Lowrie to pass. As
he did not come along, they dispersed to meet again on
Monday night following, but to their joy they learned
on Monday that a different party of men had sent Steve
Lowrie to his "long home." Although they did not kill
him, they were rejoiced to know that he was out of the
way, and that the last one of the outlaws had gone to

the "spirit land" never to return, and that the good people of Robeson county could once more breathe free and
easy.   And here the writer would say that Robeson
county owes a debt of gratitude to the noble, heroic and
self-sacrificing men who composed the Wishart company.   When they went into Scffletown to hunt the outlaws it might almost be said that the county had been
given up to the outlaws; there were few men that could
be induced in the county to take arms against them. The
county, State and United States troops had been so far
distanced and "out generalled" by these villains, that it
really seemed hopeless to attempt their capture; but the
brave men who composed the Wishart company never
faltered in their efforts to kill or capture them.   Often
were they sneered at by those who should have been
their friends; often were they turned off from the houses
of those who feared the Lowrie bandits, hungry, cold,
wet and fatigued, to seek food and shelters as best they
could; but there were five well-to-do farmers in striking
distance of Scuffletown who never failed to give them
the "best cheer" possible.   These farmers were Mr.
John McNair, Capt. Willis P. Moore, James D. Bridgers,
John McCallum, and David Townsend.   These five
were ready at any hour, day or night, to relieve their
physical wants and aid them in every possible way.
And now, as the last outlaw has run his race, and finished his course, let the good people of Robeson hold in
great remembrance "the good" done Robeson county
by the men who composed the Wishart company; let
their names be handed down to posterity, along with
those of Mr. John McNair, Capt. Willis P. Moore, James
D. Bridgers, John McCallum and David Townsend, so
that the rising generation may know who were the true

men of Robeson county during the "dark period" in her history, and during the time in which the Lowrie bandits held a bloody carnival within her borders.

STORE AND COURT HOUSE ROBBERY.

On the morning of the 19th of February, 1872, the usual quiet of the town of Lumberton was greatly disturbed by the announcement that the robber clan had been there the night before and committed robberies, but to what extent remained to be ascertained. Two of the young gentlemen of the place were out early on their way to their places of business, and discovered the iron safe from the Sheriff's office in the street, about fifty yards from the Court House. The alarm was given, the citizens aroused, and could be seen hurrying in every direction to learn who were the sufferers, and to what extent. The next thing found to be missing was a horse and dary, from the stebles of Mr. A. W. Fuller. The back door of the store of Messrs. Pope & McLeod was found open, which had been left locked and barred on the inside; on further examination they learned their safe was missing, containing a large amount of money belonging to the firm, as well as that of others which had been deposited with them for safe keeping; all their valuable papers and books were also in the safe; in addition to this, they took dry goods, ready made clothing, boots, shoes, guns, &c. They entered a blacksmith shop and took tools with which to open the safe. Messrs. Pope & McLeod immediately started out in the direction which the dray had gone, while squads of citizens were left standing about the streets consulting on

what course best to pursue. After some little time a
party was raised and started in pursuit of the robber
clan. About a-half mile from town the party pursuing
came up with Messrs. Pope & McLeod, who had found
the safe emptied of its valuable contents. The whole
party then concluded to return to Lumberton, as further pursuit would be of no avail. Several months afterwards one of the books from the store was found in a
field near Mr. McLeod's residence. A key was found
in the pocket of Tom Lowrie when killed, which fitted
the lock of the front door of the store robbed, and it
was supposed they entered the store with the false key,
locked it, and passed out through the back door. It was
the next day after their visit to Lumberton, and over
the division of that night's spoils, that Henry Berry Lowrie lost his life by the accidental discharge of his own
gun.

THE DEATH OF THE ROBBER CHIEF, HENRY
BERRY LOWRIE.

Early on the Morning of February 20th, 1872, between daylight and sunrise, the whole band of outlaws
returned to the house of Tom Lowrie after their raid on
Lumberton, having on the previous night entered the
store of Messrs. Pope & McLeod, and abstracting therefrom an iron safe, and proceeding thence to the Court
House and entering the Sheriff's office and taking along
his iron safe, proceeded forthwith to leave Lumberton
by way of the turnpike road leading across the country
by Morrisey's mill. Finding their load too heavy, they
dropped the Sheriff's safe on the streets of Lumberton
and went on with the safe of Messrs. Pope & McLeod to

a distance of about three miles and rifled it of the whole
of its contents, getting in all about twenty-two thousand
dollars. The band then wended its way to the house of
Tom Lowrie, in Scuffletown, and, being fearful of pursuit,
built up a fire near the crib of Tom Lowrie and commenced fixing their fire arms, in case they would be attacked by any party in pursuit of them; and here the outlaw chief, Henry B. Lowrie, terminated his own earthly career. Whilst attempting to draw a load out of his double
barrel gun, the gun slipping in his hand, the hammer
of one of the barrels struck against a sill of the crib and
the gun went off, the load taking effect in Henry Berry
Lowrie's face and forehead, tearing away his nose and
the greater portion of his forehead. He died almost instantly. Thus perished the great robber chief of Robeson county. Preparations were set on foot immediately
for his burial. A party of Indians went to the saw mill
of Mr. Archibald Buie for lumber, which had to be
sawed. When the lumber was obtained. Jesse Oxendine (being a carpenter) was called in and made the coffin
the other outlaws standing guard all the time. When
all the necessary preparations were completed, the remains of the dead robber chief were temporarily placed
in a shallow grave under Tom Lowrie's crib. On the
following night, near mid-night, the remaining outlaws
took up the body of the dead robber chief and carried
it off and buried it, where, in all human probability, no
white man will ever find out.

Thus passed away this remarkable bandit, in his
twenty-sixth year—the greatest scourge ever inflicted
upon the good people of Robeson county. He was said
to have had a good deal of money in his possesion at this
time, as his comrades in arms often reported to outsiders

that he was in the habit of appropriating "the lion's
share" to his own use of all the money taken, giving to
the other outlaws the other booty. No member of the
band,not even his "fidus Achates," Boss Strong, nor his
wife, Rhoda Lowrie, knew where he kept his money.
Diligent search has been made by the remaining members of the gang to find his treasure chest, but as yet,
"it is love's labor lost."   For some time after the death
of Henry Berry Lowrie. his companions denied all
knowledge of his fate; even his relations professed to
be ignorant of it, but the facts, one by one, leaked out
through different individuals of the Indian race, who
saw the dead robber chief whilst "lying in state" before
his interment.   The main object in keeping his fate concealed from the public seems to have been to keep the
timid whites in awe of the "outlaw gang," and to prevent those who were endeavoring to capture him from
getting his body.   This course of conduct on the part
of the "outlaw gang" and the Indians generally, was in accordance with their previous course.
When George Applewhite was shot, and Boss Strong
killed, they endeavored to divert public attention by
telling various tales in regard to the fate of each, in
in which there was not one particle of truth; but now,
at this writing, inasmuch as Steve Lowrie, the last outlaw, has also gone to the "spirit land," and the reign of
the gang terminated, and there being no need of mystery
in regard to the fate of the robber chief; several Indians
in Scuffletown are outspoken in regard to the manner in
which Henry Berry Lowrie met his fate, and they all
verify the facts as above recited.   This noted Indian
bandit is certainly gone to the criminal's bourne; he is
most certainly done making raids on the law-abiding

citizens of Robeson county; he is assuredly done frightening the women and children of the white race by his
martial appearance; his scepter has been laid aside and
his spirit summoned to appear before "the Judge of all
the earth," to answer for the long catalog of crimes, as
long, probably, as the list of Homer's ships. Some have
compared him to Oceola, or Powell, the noted leader of
the Seminole Indians in Florida, others to "the bold
archer" Robin Hood, whilst still others say that he
was more like Rob Roy McGregor. Be this as it may, he
certainly played an extended role in his own way, being the leader of the most formidable band of outlaws,
considering the smallness of its numbers, that has ever
appeared in this country. He developed a cunning,
bloodthirstiness, and courage unmatched in the history
of his race.

THE KILLING OF ANDREW STRONG.

Mr. William Wilson, a native of Guilford county,
aged thirty-eight, being in the employ of A. & W. Mc-
Queen, incurred by some means or other, the displeasure
of Steve Lowrie and Andrew Strong, the only two remaining outlaws. Sometime in the month of December, 1872, therefore, Steve Lowrie, and Andrew Strong,
on the morning of December 25, 1872, went to the store
of Mr. John Humphrey at Pates, a station on the Carolina Central Railway, in the heart of Scuffletown,
where Mr. William Wilson was a clerk, and informed
him that he had been talking about them. Mr. Wilson
did not say much, one way or the other, whereupon Andrew Strong told Mr. Wilson "that he would give him
until train time the next day to leave the county, and

that if he did not leave, that he (Andrew Strong) would
kill him;" they then left Pates, heavily armed on a
Christmas Frolic. Mr. Wilson, after their departure,
loaded up a double-barrel shot-gun with buck-shot, and
concealed it under a coverlet in an adjoining room for
use whenever the outlaws would make their appearance.
So about 4 o'clock p. m., on the same day, Andrew
Strong alone made his appearance again at the store of
Mr. John Humphrey. and after purchasing a few articles
of merchandise, turned and walked out on the piazza in
front of the shore, and leaning up against a post with his
back towards the door of the store, Mr. Wilson deliber-
ately fired on him, the shot taking effect in the neck of
the outlaw, killing him almost instantly. Several Indians being present, Mr. Wilson informed them that
whoever touched or laid his hand on the body of Andrew Strong, he would kill him instantly with the other
barrel of his shot-gun, which was then cocked: he then
pressed a wagon and a pair of mules and compelled John
Humphrey, Floyd Oxendine and two other Indians,
(names not recollected) to place the body of Andrew
Strong in the wagon and accompany him, with the remains of the dead outlaw, to Lumberton, where the
whole party arrived sometime after nightfall, and formally delivered the body of Andrew Strong to the Sheriff
of the county, who identified it as the body of Andrew
Strong. and paid forthwith the reward which had been
offered for the body of Andrew Strong, dead or alive,
and fixed up the papers for Mr. Wilson to draw from
the State Treasury the amount offered by the State,
which amount the State Treasurer paid Mr. Wilson as
soon as he presented the papers. Thus perished Andrew Strong. another of the Robeson county outlaws.

He was the elder brother of Boss Strong, and was in his
twenty-fourth year.   He was a little over six feet high,
tall and slim, and nearly white; he possessed beard
somewhat of a reddish color, and had dark straight hair
on his head.   He was the Oily Gammon of the "outlaw
gang," and could wear a look of great meekness, and,
whilst at the same time, his tongue was soft and treacherous, so much so, that it would seem difficult for sugar
or butter to melt in his mouth.   The civil authorities had
him up once in Court and when the Solicitor in behalf of the
State read out the indictment, his great soft eyes seemed
as if ready to shed tears at such unjust imputations.   He
married the daughter of Henry Sampson, another Indian of Scuffletown.   Andrew Strong was a cowardly
sneak; when he would kill a person the honey would
almost seem to drop from his tongue into the wound he
had inflicted; indeed he might be called a professor of
deceit, perfidious, plausible, uncertain, deadly — he was
certainly the meanest of the gang.

————

A NIGHT AMONG THE ROBBERS.

About the middle of November 1870, a detective who
had been employed to watch the movements of the
Lowrie gang of this county, established a camp in a bay
near Moss Neck for the purpose of prosecuting his mis-
sion with as much secrecy as possible.   The camp was
near the house of Mr. W. C. McNeill, one of the best
citizens of our county; and his son Malcom was in the
habit of visiting the camp occasionally, and giving Mr.
Sanders such assistance as he could.   On Sunday, the
20th of November, he met with three young men whom

he knew to be reliable, made an engagement to meet them
after night at the camp of Mr. Sanders.   The young men
accordingly repaired to the camp about 4 o'clock in the
afternoon to await the arrival of Mr. McNeill, who did
not reach the camp until about 7'oclock p. m.   The following is Mr. McNeill's statement of what occurred on
his approach to the camp:

"When I approached within a short distance of the
camp, I saw the young men I was to meet there.   They
immediately informed me that the camp was surrounded by the robbers, and that if I attempted to escape, I would be shot, I halted and made a movement
to draw my pistol, when four men arose among the
bushes, and presenting their cocked guns, warned me
that I was a prisoner, and that I would be fired upon if
I did not immediately surrender.   These men I recognized as Henry B. Lowrie, Stephen Lowrie, George
Applewhite and Boss Strong.   H. B. took my repeater
from me, saying that I might make myself at home, as
they would take care of me that night.   I then took my
position with the other prisoners around the camp fire;
but after a short time H. B. Lowrie summoned me to
go with him a short distance from the camp; he then
turned and addressed me in the following language:
"G—d d—n your soul, I want to know where Sanders
is. You know all about him; a respectable white man, and
one you do not suspect, has told me you are harboring
him, and doing all you can to assist him in hunting us
down.   I'm straight on your track now, G—d d—n
you, and if you don't tell all about Sanders, I'll kill you
right here; I intend to kill you anyhow, as soon as we
get Sanders."   He asked me when I saw Sanders.   I replied, last Saturday week.   He then escorted me back

to the camp, and very soon Stephen Lowrie took me
out for a chat; he asked me about the same questions as
Henry B. had, and received the same answers—he also
made the same threats, and charged me with harboring
Sanders. We passed the whole night in the camp—the
prisoners occupying Sanders' quarters (Mr. Sanders
was absent at the time), and the robbers stationed around
us. During the night Stephen Lowrie exhibited to me a
pack of cards, which he said he bought at the Scotch
Fair, and boasted of his boldness in visiting that place.
Messengers were sent at intervals through the night in
two different directions from the camp, apparently to
confer with parties stationed a short distance off. About
daylight the robbers became impatient, and began to
look out as for the arrival of some one whom they expected to come in at that hour. Soon after daylight
Stephen Lowrie went out alone in the direction of Moss
Neck; after he had been gone about ten minutes, I heard
several voices a short distance from the camp cry, "halt!"
One of them I recognized as the voice of Stephen Lowrie, the others of the men whom I had not seen in the
camp; I also heard a voice which I recognized to be
that of Sanders say, "I surrender." Henry B. Lowrie,
George Applewhite and Henderson Oxendine now left
us and ran out in the direction of the voices, leaving us
in charge of Boss Strong. H. B. and Stephen Lowrie
returned to the camp singing and rejoicing, saying that
they had got the buck they wanted. H. B. Lowrie then
approached me and said, "G—d d—n you, will you tell
a straight tale now? You said you hadn't seen Sanders
since Saturday week—d—n you, you saw him last Saturday." Stephen Lowrie then took me aside and said,

"Henry Berry is mad with you—he is mad enough to kill you, and I am afraid he will kill you, but I'll try to prevent it." Henry Berry then called me aside and said, "Now, G—d d—n you, you've been doing all you could against me—you've been harboring this man Sanders and trying to have us captured —I've got a notion to kill you right here, but if you'll promise me to leave the country I believe I'll let you off this time, but if I ever get hold of you again, you may look out." He then returned the pistols that had been taken from the other prisoners, but he kept mine, saying he would take care of it.   He then told me he would give me a little advice: "I might go to Moss Neck and run my shebang—I might have a guard there if I wished, but he would advise me to leave the country, and leave immediately."   Said he, "You are young, stout, healthy, and able to do good business; I hate to interfere with you, but you have done so much against us, I've got a notion to kill you.   Tell your father if he will stay at home and let us alone he needn't be afraid, but he must walk a chalk line."   They then sent me and the other young men they had captured off in one direction, and they moved off in an opposite direction.   I did not see Sanders, as he was not brought into the camp, but I recognized his voice in pronouncing the words "I surrender," when halted near the camp.

STEPHEN LOWRIE.

We now come to the closing scene of outlawry in Robeson county—when the last desperado of that formidable "Lowrie Band" played his own death march on the eve of joining his faithful comrades in crime and

bloodshed who had gone on before to judgment and justice.   No tongue can picture or pen portray the great
sense of relief that swelled in many bosoms at the announcement that "the last outlaw is dead."   No more
will suffering mothers and wives, on seeing their loved
ones depart for their places of business, offer up the
heartfelt prayer, "God protect our dear son or husband
from the rage of Steve Lowrie;" never again shall his
swarthy face peer into our dwellings, sending a thrill of
horror through our veins, and causing our hearts to
stand still with fear and apprehension ; no more shall the
echo of his rifle reverberate through field and forest :-his
old haunts are desolate; the well beaten paths through
swamp and woodland are overgrown with briar and
bramble; his cabin, own deserted, stands crumbling in
decay, reminding the passer-by that the reign of terror
is over in Robeson—the glory of the robber chief and
his clan is ended, and naturally a prayer of thanksgiv-
ing arises for the long hoped-for deliverance,

Steve Lowrie was about six feet high, well proportioned, carrying his head a little forward, giving him
the appearance of being slightly stoop-shouldered.   He
was always well armed with navy repeaters, a Henry
rifle and occasionally a double barrel gun.   After the
killing of the other members of the band, and he was
left the field to himself, he remained for several months
very quiet.   He finally began to grow weary of the
hum-drum, inactive life he was leading, and he was grad-
ually becoming troublesome.   He drank a good deal,
and in his drinking hours was really dangerous.   He
made many threats, particularly while drinking, as to
what he intended doing were he not pardoned, and asserted positively that he had boys drilling, and as soon

as they equalled him in markmanship they would start
out, and the past was not a circumstance to that which
was in store for those whom he believed to be his enemies.   Several times within a few days before he was
killed he mentioned the names of three young men in
the neighborhood that he had decided to kill in a few
days.   One of them was Mr. Patterson, who aided in
ridding the county of his vile presence on the memorable night of the 23rd of February, 1874.   Some of his
own color stood in much fear of him, as he had whipped
some of their wives and daughters severely, and threatened killing them if he heard of their talking about him
again.

Although he strode from place to place, apparently at
ease and without fear, his paths were watched.   It was
no easy matter, though it may appear so to those unacquainted with the real facts in the case, to come up with
him.   Those who were eagerly in pursuit of him,
found it difficult to locate him.   To-day he might
be at the house of one of his many friends for a few
hours; it might be weeks before he would visit the same
place again.   A few weeks before he was killed, a party
of three who had been lying in wait for hours near the
house of a colored man, where he was known to call
very often in passing, had the pleasure of seeing him
emerge from the house and take his place for a chat in
such a position as to give them an opportunity of giving
him a taste of powder, but they, so eager for the game,
fired too hasty—and missed.   He ran and made good
his escape unhurt, amid a shower of shot.   This warning made him more cautious, and led him to avoid such
places in future.   He left that portion of the neighborhood and went higher up, where in a few weeks he met

his just doom at the hands of the young men whose names will appear in the following particulars :

The families of Messrs. D. Holcomb and Davis Bullard were frequently annoyed by the visits of Steve Lowrie. It was at the house of the father of Davis (Mr. E. Bullard) that the two young men above named met Steve in December, 1873, and jointly resolved to take his life or rid their families of his company. They accordingly left the house and proceeded to station themselves on the road which they supposed he would go on his way home. Steve remained until about 9 o'clock and left, taking the direction in which the boys had gone, but before getting to them took a by-path, thus escaping them. Several weeks after this, Mr. Holcomb was on his way to Red Banks, a depot on the Carolina Central Railway, when he was met and accosted by Steve. He inquired of Mr. H. where he was going. He told him, and in turn made the same inquiry of Steve. He replied that he was going over to a whiskey wagon that had camped a short distance off. Each then went on his way. In the afternoon of the same day, as Mr. H. was returning from the Banks, he again met Steve, in company with the wagon that he had spoken of in the morning. He told Mr. Holcomb that he must go back with him a mile or so to McLaughlin's (the mother of the notorious Zach. McLaughlin) to borrow a jug to put some whiskey in, which he had bought from the wagoner. When they reached McLaughlin's Steve asked Mr. Holcomb if he brought any letters from the office. He told him that he had one for Mr. Purcell. He desired Mr. H. to open and read the letter to him. This he refused, telling him that if he would go to Mr. Purcell's he

would read it for him.   He readily consented to do this,
requesting Mr. H. to accompany him.   He mounted Mr.
Holcomb's horse, compelling him to take a seat behind
him.   Mr. Holcomb objected to this style of riding, and
proposed to go to Mr. Bullard's and borrow another animal, to which he assented.   Mr. H. had another object
in view in going to this place, which Steve did not suspect.   While he was getting another animal he was also
laying a plan with Mr. Thomas Bullard to go and get
his brother Robert Holcomb to waylay the road, and on
their return to pick Lowrie off; but he again frustrated
them by taking a by-way.   When they reached Mr.
Purcell's and the letter was handed him, Steve remarked that his business there was to know the contents of
that letter.   It was read to him, but it was not concerning the petition for his pardon, as he thought, and which
was the cause of his showing so much interest in it.   After leaving Mr. Purcell's, Steve went to the house of Mr.
Holcomb and remained about one hour.   Davis Bullard
was also there, and Steve told him and Mr. H. that they
must go to the house of a Mr. Jones that lived near, and
get him some chickens.   They started, but instead of
going to Mr. Jones', they went to Mr. Patterson's,
called him out, told him the situation, and requested him
to go with him.   Before starting they went to the fowl-
house and took a chicken, in order to disarm Steve of
any suspicion which might arise in his mind from their
prolonged stay.   They had parted with Steve at a negro house, and on their return were to go with him to
the house of Purcell Locklear, where there was a whiskey wagon camped.   Mr. Patterson left them to conceal
himself on the road until they would pass, and he was
then to go on to the wagon.   Steve being ever on the

alert, would have at once suspected some scheme if Mr.
P. had gone in company with them. Their object in
getting Mr. P. to go with them was to assist in ridding
the county then and there of the last outlaw, should op-
portunity offer. The boys were all unarmed, but Mr.
H. picked up an axe, intending to kill him with it, but
Steve turned suddenly, and again they were thwarted.
Seeing no prospect of a chance that night, they left,

About two weeks after this, Steve was again at Mr.
E. Bullard's, and stayed until after supper. As soon
as Davis learned that he was at the house of his father,
he went after Mr. Holcomb to go with him to waylay
the road, hoping to be more successful. They stationed
themselves on the road, taking their stand behind the
posts of a gate to await his coming. This time they
were doomed to disappointment, for in passing the gate
he walked so near the post as to render it impossible to
bring their guns to bear upon him. A short time after
this, Mr. Holcomb heard of him in the neighborhood,
and got Mr. Sutton to go with him to endeavor to learn
his whereabouts; they concluded to get Mr. Patterson
also, and went to his house for that purpose. Davis
Bullard had also heard of him, and had been before
them, and he, in company with Mr. Patterson, had gone
to try and intercept him. As they were not sufficiently supplied with ammunition, they went to the house of
Mr. H. to supply themselves. When they came near
the house they heard some one picking the banjo; on
waiting a short time they learned it was Steve. They
were confident that the other boys were somewhere in
the vicinity, and walked around to see if they could get
together. They soon found them, and together took
their places near a hay-loft, where Steve had slept

sometime before.   They sat there until near 11 o'clock,
when they concluded he would not remain all night,
and changed their position over near the road that he
would take should he go home.   In a few minutes he
came out and went into the loft, passing in a few feet
of their first stand.   They gave up the chase for this
time, but with the determination to try again whenever
opportunity offered.

Friday night before he was killed•the following Monday there was a social gathering at the house of Mr.
Neill Patterson.   Two of the boys present walked out;
a short distance from the house some one hailed them,
which proved to be Steve Lowrie.   He conversed with
them a short time, and during the conversation laugh-
ed so loudly as to be heard at the house.   Messrs. Mc.
Patterson and Davis Bullard were sitting at the time
out in the yard laying a plan to kill him.   They heard
and recognized his voice.   Davis walked out and took
him to one side to have a private chat with him, and to
learn if possible where he might be for a day or two.
He proposed to Steve to make up a party somewhere
in the neighborhood and they would have some fun.
Steve readily agreed, and appointed one to be at Hugh
McLean's the following Tuesday night.   He told Davis
he must be sure and attend, told him who to invite,
and to speak of it to no one else, and particularly to
keep it a secret from Mc. Patterson and John Bridgers.
He then left.   The next day Mr. T. Bullard and Mc.
Patterson were at the Banks.   There were also two
whiskey wagons.   The above gentlemen heard the
wagoners say they intended camping at Martin Mc-
Nair's (colored) that night and until the following

Monday. They came home. reported the same to
Messrs. Holcomb and Davis Bullard, and they laid
plans accordingly ; they knew that Steve was in the
habit of visiting the wagons that camped at this
place. The day following (being Sunday) they were
to meet at church and mature their plans. Messrs.
Holcomb and Bullard did not return to their own
homes, but went to the house of a neighbor in order to
slip up to the wagon after dark without any one's becoming aware of their plans except their own party.
After dark they crept up in about fifty yards of the
wagoner's camp to learn if Steve was there. A loud
laugh rang out on the stillness of the night which they
at once recognized as Steve Lowrie's. They were sure
of the game now; they fully intended this night, to end
the drama; the following day should herald to an outraged people the end of outlawry in Robeson. The
brave fellows who had dogged his footsteps and wisely
kept their own counsel, proceeded to the house of Mr.
E. Bullard to procure their arms. Here they found
Messrs. Patterson and Sutton. They did not have
guns sufficient to arm a party of four, and Mr. Holcomb proposed to Davis to lend his gun to Mr. Sutton
and he (Davis) to go to the wagon, and keep a bright fire,
and also to arrange so as to give them a chance of a
fair trial of their skill at the outlaw. Davis, only a boy
of eighteen, being so eager for the fray, at first refused;
the others insisted, as Steve had more confidence in Davis
than any of their party, and had never been known to
evince any anger or to express a doubt with regard to
him. It being necessary that some one cognizant of their
plan should be in company with Steve in order to suc-

ceed, Davis finally consented, and at once proceeded
to the wagon before the other boys took their places.
Messrs. Holcomb and Sutton selected their position inside of a fence on the opposite side of the road from the
wagon, and about twenty-five yards distant.   They
learned at once that they had an excellent opportunity
of singling Steve out from the balance of the Indians and
negroes, about a dozen of whom were also at the wagon.
Mr. Holcomb raised his gun to take aim, when Mr. Sutton remarked that he had lost the cap from his gun.
Mr. H. then took a cap from his own gun, split it so as
to fit a musket and handed it to him, but he (Mr. S.) was
so excited that he dropped it.   Being now without caps,
they had to go to Mr. Bullard's (one-fourth of a mile) to
get some, after which they returned to their position.
Here they waited some time without an opportunity of
a shot, and being tired, crawled off some little distance
and lay down to rest.   On going back, they overheard
Steve making a plan to take some of the crowd and go
to Mr. John McNair's to get some chickens; they then
decided to go and waylay the road to Mr. McNair's and
shoot him as he passed.   There they waited some time,
and as they did not go on, concluded that the party had
gone another way.   They started back to ascertain, and
met Messrs. Tom Bullard and Charlie Holcomb.   They
informed them that Steve was still at the wagon.   And
it was their impression that he intended remaining. The
boys all went on to Mr. E. Bullard's and requested Mr.
Patterson to go home and get his gun and go back to
their old stand.   He at once, in company with Mr. Sutton, went after his gun, and Mr. Holcomb returned to
his former position alone, to await their return.   Mr.

Tom Bullard went to the wagon to try and learn what was to be the order of the night. In the meantime, Messrs. Patterson and Sutton joined Mr. Holcomb, and together, they were awaiting Mr. Bullard's report; he came in a few moments, reporting that Steve had sent for his "banjo," and without doubt would remain at the wagon all night, and he also learned that Steve had, with a party of several, been to Mr. McNair's, entered his fowl-house by breaking three locks and brought six chickens and a large turkey to the wagon; the chickens had been cooked and eaten—the turkey was on cooking for breakfast. He compelled Davis Bullard to accompany him to Mr. McNair's. Steve was a firm believer in conjuration, and kept on hand a supply of roots, bones, &c.; before he started after the chickens, he took something from his pocket, put it in a bottle of whiskey, and after shaking well together, anointed his person with it, remarking at the time with an oath, that there was not a man in the State that could hit him with a shot. The party, after hearing this report, proceeded to their old stand near the fence. They discovered Steve sitting with his head down, putting his banjo in tune, and determined as soon as he would raise his head that they would fire. In a moment he threw his head back and commenced his tune, when simultaneously the guns fired which ended his career on earth, and sent him, a blood-stained, crime-hardened wretch, to answer before a great tribunal for the deeds committed while in the flesh. With a deep groan, he fell forward lifeless, without warning. As he measured to others, even so was it meted out to him. They at once made arrangements to carry his body to Lumberton, where it was delivered to the

Sheriff, amid the shouts and acclamations of a large crowd. It being court week in Lumberton, the Judge was there, and in his charge highly commended the young men for their praise-worthy act.

Their papers to obtain the reward placed upon his head being duly made out, signed and delivered to them, Messrs. Patterson and Sutton took the cars for Raleigh, where they received the sum offered for the body of Stephen Lowrie—the last outlaw in Robeson.

The above was taken from a photograph of the widow of Stephen Lowrie, who still lives (1909).

FROM THE FAYETTEVILLE EAGLE OF FEB-RUARY 26, 1874.

Perhaps no people have been so scourged as the people of Robeson, nevertheless they have been abused and villified. The dandified clerk in the city counting-room would say, "Why don't those people rise up and extirpate the Lowrie gang? If I was there, I could very easily stop this thing." The stroller along the side-walks made similar remarks. Even dignified and cautious people sometimes made censorious remarks of Robeson county. A multitude of talkers afar off from the terrible scenes enacted by this Lowrie band had this and that to say about the good people of Robeson county. Curt, petulant and sarcastic sayings passed from the mouths of bomb-proof assailants, but through it all, the killing went on. Not one of the captious critics of Robeson suffered one iota in purse or person. They were afar off, although sometimes trembling. We take this opportunity, the killing of the last outlaw, to say to the country at large, what we know to be strictly true, that there is no more courageous, industrious, whole-souled people in the world than the citizens of Robeson, and all through the Lowrie war, whether under the command of a United States officer or the Sheriff, they conducted themselves with courage and a high sense of public duty. The obstacles these people had to encounter in suppressing the Lowrie gang is not a property of the bomb-proof critic or the side-walk loafer, but it is the province of truth and history to delineate these facts.

* APPENDIX.

DECENDANTS OF THE LOST COLONY—STRANGE BLENDING
OF INDIAN AND WHITE—THEIR SCHOOL—THEIR CHAR-
ARTERISTICS AND SOME TYPES OF THE RACE.

I shall never forget the very curious sensation I ex-
perienced as I stood on a wagon in the centre of more
than a thousand of the Croatans, at their Normal School
at Pate's, in Robeson county, and spoke to them in May.
Just a month before I had been at Roanoke Island and
at that classic spot, Fort Raleigh, and had gone to the
edge and standing on the crest of a sand-dune there, between two wind-tossed live oaks, had looked out across
the yellow waters of the narrow sound at the banks beyond, which separate the sound from the sea, and looking further eastward yet, had seen the heaving water of
the ocean, stretching three thousand miles away and
more, towards that England for which the deserted,
lonely and terror-stricken third colony of Sir Walter
Raleigh must have yearned so hopelessly, in the closing
years of that fateful experiment at settlement which the
great Knight made in this State of ours.

A STRANGE BLENDING.

As I looked into the faces of one of the most attentive
audiences possible and saw that strange blending of Indian and white, my mind went back through the mist of
years and there came the reflection that there were no
stranger people on the continent than those before me.

* Written by Col. F. A. Old, of Raleigh, N. C. Col. Olds visited
that section of Rebeson County in which the Croatan Indians live,
and wrote a series of newspaper articles as a result of his visit.
This appendix contains these articles in condensed form.

The Croatans owe to one man, Hamilton McMillan, their status in North Carolina; their status which forbids inter marriage except among themselves; which makes them a tribe, and in a way the wards of the State; just as the Cherokees of the Eastern Band; in the mountain region, who have about the same numerical strength, are the wards of the Nation.   The Cherokees, however, have had far more done for them than have the Croatans.

These Croatans were found by the earliest people who pushed up into North Carolina northward from the Charleston settlement to be a blend of Indian and English; to have extremely neat houses though of logs; extraordinarily good roads for that period; well-kept yards, and to have many peculiarities of Old English speech. Ever since that time those peculiarities have existed, and they stand broadly out now.   In fact the Croatans are marked as a peculiar people.   No white man on earth knows them nearly so well as Hamilton McMillan, of Red Springs, who, when in the Legislature of 1887, brought about their official recognition by the State, securing a small appropriation for the normal school and giving them absolutely separate schools, under a distinct system.

ROUTE TO INDIAN COUNTRY.

This much by way of preface. The route into this Indian country runs through the fertile section west of Lumberton and the lands were found as flat as a floor, with very dark soil and with streams which have all the clearness marking those which traverse the cypress and juniper region.

That part of the State has many characteristics of ex-

The above illustration shows the Normal School building at Pates. This house has been standing for some years. As proof of their appreciation of what the State is doing for them in regard to education they have purchased a tract of land at Pembroke, which is situated about a mile from the present school site, on which they are now (1909) erecting a large modern school building.

treme eastern North Carolina and these Indians, when
they originally removed from the mainland, in what is
now Hyde county and thereabouts, must have found
the section very home-like indeed.

THE NORMAL SCHOOL.

It was a short walk along the railway track to the
normal school, a building half unpainted and standing
on the edge of a pine grove, with a church to one side,
and in the rear one of the public schools of this race,
which is so thickset in the country of which Pate's is the
centre, for, in a small radius the bulk of the Croatans
live. In the school were gathered the students, about
70 in number, and their tints ran all the way from the
deep copper color of the Indian to almost perfect white.
Beautiful hair and extremely fine eyes was the rule
and not the exception and they carried themselves well.
In a little talk the writer introduced himself and told the
purpose of his visit, which was to see them in their home
and school life.   They were very kind in their recep-
tion and presently Preston Locklear, a very striking type
of their people, drove up his buggy and we made ready
to make a trip through their settlements.   Locklear explained that his name had become corrupted from
Lockyer, which is very distinctly English.   We got pictures of the house, or rather two houses, occupied by
Mr. Jacobs, near the school, the people being of the pronounced Croatan type, the house being extremely well
built of logs, with a wonderful clean yard of shining
sand, with abounding shrubbery and trees, and with a
well curbed with a cypress log and having an old-fash-
ioned and long sweep.   Mr. Jacobs' mother is the widow
of one of the oldest Methodist preachers.

The next place visited was the home of Harriet Graham, a cozy little cabin, with a garden adjoining, the house of logs, and the furniture all hand-made, and the surroundings looking very Indian-like indeed. As guides there went with us two Croatan girls.

Locklear said his son was a doctor and had been out in the Indian Territory and was at once recognized by the Indians there as being of their race of people. He said his son had graduated at Baltimore.

WASHINGTON LOWERY.

The third place visited was the most striking of all; this being the home of the venerable Washington Lowery, or Lowrie, known far and near among his people as "Uncle Wash". His home, built of logs like the rest, embraces several buildings, and there was a porch of unique design, also of logs. The old man was partially paralyzed, but he talked very well indeed. He had a good deal to say about his people and said he had heard his "feyther" and "grand-feyther" speak over and over again about their having come from Roanoke Island. He said there was no doubt about the orgin of his people, and seemed to be very proud of it indeed. He referred to the fact that he had been out in the Indian Territory a good many years ago and said he had looked into the question of citizenship or tribeship there and that the Indians had recognized him as of their people, but that their chiefs wanted his papers to show whence he came. "Uncle Wash" was seated in a home-made chair, the seat of which was of cowskin with the hair on, and all about inside and out were home-made furniture and appliances, old-time things, spinning-

wheels, looms, etc., and his wife brought out home made
cloth for winter and summer use.   Her name is Kather-
ine and some of the cloth of jeans, brown in color, which
she had made, she said she had dyed with walnut
leaves.   Then there was homespun of several colors,
some of it dyed with indigo, which has been raised on
the place for generations.   We went all through this
Lowery home, in one great room being four beds, but
the walls being quite open, so that there was plenty of ventilation.   Lowery said he was kin to
the Cherokees in this State and that all his people were;
that he had known this close kinship always and that
he had told the Cherokee and Creek Indians, when he
had visited them in their own territory about this, and
that they had received him well.   He said he had gone
to the Territory the "year of the shake," by this meaning in 1886, when the great earth-quake shocks were
felt.   That was the year before the Croatans were given
citizenship.   Lowery said that most of the Croatan
houses were in the style of his, but some double houses
were seen with rooms right and left, and a broad open
space between, all under one roof.   Such houses as
these used to be common in the North Carolina mountains.

It was learned that they felt very proud of how well
they had preserved themselves as a people, in view of
the fact that the constitution of 1835, which took away
from everybody except the whites the right to vote, had
put them beyond the pales and made them virtually
Ishmaelites.   Under such conditions no race could have
preserved its purity better than the Croatans.   There
are people, some even in Robeson county perhaps, who

speak of the Croatans as if they were negroes, but never
was there anything further from the truth.

THE INDIAN TRAITS.

They have the Indian traits of suspicion and of
revenge. I had been among the Indians in western
North Carolina and standing there amidst these people,
could not help thinking that if they could pay a visit to
their Cherokee brethren they would be greeted as of
their very own people. Yet as a race they know nothing
about the Cherokees. Cut off from everything, for so
many years, for they had always voted up to 1835, they
are entitled to wonderful credit for what they have
done. Now they all vote under the "grandfather clause".
They used to be largely Republicans, but are now
mainly Democrats. In years past politicians sought to
use them.

It is in language construction that the teachers find
the greatest trouble with them. They have so many
old phrases and such old pronunciation of not a few
words that a friend remarked that they talked almost
exactly like the people in some English countries. Upon
the roll of the pupils in schools were names borne by
the Roanoke colonists. Assurances were given that
these people had made as much relative improvement
in the past 25 years as any others in their section of
the State or in any other part of it, yet they started at
zero. Of course there is plenty of room for further improvement. They are domestic in their life and they
need only two things, these being abstention from liquor
and the cultivation of a higher standard of morals in
home life. They have been the prey of designing white
men, who have gone in their section for evil purposes

these many years. This and their past treatment by the whites have been the chief difficulties in securing their confidence. The lack of relics and tradition among them is most impressive, but yet what have the Cherokees in western North Carolina to show now of the old days except what the burial mounds contain? In the eastern part of the State the Indians have so faded away that they are not even a memory, the last remnant of them having been in Bertie county.

LOVE GAY CLOTHING.

Another Indian trait is the love for bright clothing. I have seen this in the West and also among the North Carolina Cherokees and among the Florida Seminoles. Red, blue and yellow are the delight particularly of the girls. The beauty of the girls was a subject of general comment, most having straight hair, dense black, but in some cases it curled gracefully.

In the old times these people used to work a great deal in the turpentine and lumber interests but these have largely passed away. The negroes do not like the Croatans. There are very few negroes in the Croatan country.

HOME OF RHODA LOWERY.

Rhoda Lowery, the widow of Henry Berry Lowery, who, in 1870, was the terror of that part of the State. Those were in the old days when Maxton, now so thriving a town and making such a brave show along the railway, was but a straggling village and was called Shoe Heel, (a corruption of Quhele, it seems). Those were the times when the Croatan Indian settlement was known as Scuffletown. That was a corruption too, for in the long-ago it was "Scoville Town", taking its name from a family of the tribe which was prominent.   At the time of our visit there was not a suggestion of age in Rhoda's face, form or hair, and it seemed hard to realize that she had figured 38 years ago and must be well on toward 60.   One would have guessed something around 40 as her age.   Her father was a Yankee and her mother a Sweet, the latter being a family in South Carolina, living in a place where there are several of the Croatan families, one of these having formerly been the Dirigos, though this is corrupted into quite another name.   Rhoda spoke of Henry Berry Lowery as the handsomest man she ever saw.   She has several acres of ground and raises on this everything she needs.

The Croatans are no believers in race suicide, Joseph Locklear had twenty-five children, one wife being the mother of them all.   Another woman, Missouri Locklear, who is only 28 years old and has eleven children, there being two sets of twins. Large families are the rule and it was a sight to see the farm wagons and other vehicles coming to the commencement, packed with children, these looking like animated bouquets, as far as the girls were concerned, so gay were the colors of dresses, hats and sashes.   There are some two thousand school children of these people and there are seven hundred voters.   They voted always until 1838, and then were deprived of the ballot until 1868, being nearly twenty years before the time when they were set apart by the State as a separate people.   No one knows exactly the number of them, but there are pretty close to 3,500.   Some of them raise as many as 75 bales of cotton.   More of them are Baptist than of other denominations, most of the remainder belonging to the Northern

Methodist Church.   There is a number of preachers among them.

The word "mon", an old English form of "man", was heard over and over again and one of the chiefs said that a favorite gesture and phrase of some of the Croatans, when excited, was to strike the palm of one hand with the fist and say: "Dom my hand to the bone".   It is said that this was quite an oath in some parts of England a long time ago and yet obtains there.   The names Lowery, Locklear, Oxendine, Dial, Bullard, Sampson, Brooks and Chavis were heard, those of Locklear and Lowery predominating.   It was found that the Raleigh colonists names of Lowery, Sampson, Harris, Jones, Brooks and Chavis were matched by the students, while in the community the names of a score of the white colonists are perpetuated.   A subject furnished by this community for a poem which if properly wrought out would surpass in pathos David's story of the dispersion of the Jews or Long Fellow's "Evangeline".   To tell the truth, down under the surface there was just a tinge of sadness in these people.   Not all the white people are friends to these Croatans.   The more pronounced type of Croatan, the more solemn and dignified they are and as stoical as any red man.

COUNTRY NEEDS DRAINAGE.

The great need of the country of the Croatans is good drainage.   A lot of it is in swamp.   As a matter of fact a county drainage system for Robeson county, giving an opportunity for cross drainage would be a grand investment.   The land is good to work and the crops show it. The normal school house stands in the very centre of what used to be "Scuffletown".   Mention has been

made of the isolation of these people.   There was, years
ago a marriage of a Croatan woman to a negro, this
having occurred before the recognition of the race in 1887.
This was followed by an arrest and conviction.

The Lumber river, one of the most striking streams
in the lower section of the State, runs through the heart
of the Croatan country.   The river is entirely fed by
springs and is bordered by cypress and juniper, which
give it the tint of such eastern streams as the Pasquotank
river, for example, intensely dark in the mass, but very
clear in a small quantity, and extremely palatable as
drinking water.   This was another similarity between
the section where these people are settled and that from
whence their ancestors came.

GROWERS OF GRAPES.

Almost every house has nearby it a scuppernong vine
and nowhere in this State is this grape finer.   Of all the
grapes this one is the best liked by these people.   When
asked if any of them had ever visited Roanoke island
the reply was made none except the Revels family.
These went to the island and the site of the old fort a
good many years ago before the site was marked.   They
went to various places in that section, on the banks and
on the mainland.   Revels was a United States Senator
from Mississippi and was classed as a colored man, the
Croatan not then having any distinct status.

The Croatans increase very rapidly in numbers under
sanitary conditions, and must soon become important
factors for good or evil in that part of the State.   The
intelligent and leading men among them are very hope-
ful for the future and the interest the State has manifest-
ed in their educational progress lately is arousing general

interest, if not enthusiasm, as an illustration of which they have themselves purchased, near Pembroke ten acres of land, upon which to erect a better school building. While many of them own land, none of them are wealthy. Without aid from the State their educational progress must still be retarded by many diffi cult problems. They are not able themselves to provide such a school as they need and the fostering care of the State is their hope. Their speech and manners have always marked them as a peculiar people. Of course they still feel deeply the injustice done them by the laws of 1835, which forced nearly all the older men and women into involuntary ignorance, but they now fully realize the meaning to their prosperity of the State's effort to aid them in educating their children.

BECOMING GOOD CITIZENS.

Many persons have been told that the Croatans are all revengeful and hate the whites. This was a wrong impression. Those who have been educated at schools are now, almost without exception, among the best citizens of the Croatans. Whiskey and bad white men were once the curse of the Croatan people, but here there is a rapid and radical change; a large part of the Croatan vote was cast for prohibition. The law of 1835 closed to these people every avenue of hope and said in effect that they must submit to being absorbed by the negro race. Their white neighbors withdrew many privileges which had previously been granted them. It must be borne in mind that this intolerable condition existed for over fifty years. The Croatans have very quick perceptions, distinguishing readily between a flatterer and a friend, and they say frankly that they hold the former in contempt, and esteem the latter highly.

QUEER OLD REMEDIES.

It was found that these people use remedies at least which were prescribed in English medical works as far back as 1706, and one of these is so singular that it deserves to be recorded, it being three live lice in a drink of whiskey, it being esteemed two hundred years ago and now as a sovereign for fever. Thus while there are a few traditions, things are handed down. I have no doubt that houses look now as they did say 200 years ago or more. Certainly in no parts of the State except among the Cherokees and a few of the whites in the wilder portions of the mountains, are there so many home-made things. The houses simply abound with them. These people are good shots and when they do shoot usually kill. One lady at Pembroke still carries in her body a ball from the gun of Henry Lowery, who fired it at her father. They love to fish and hunt. The shades of color are as varied as one can see in a walk in Mexico, and some of the pronounced Indian faces are wonderfully like those of the Mexican Indians (not the peons), while others for tint and outline will compare with those in a white community. The eyes are really the haunting things. There are some women of ill repute and there are some who sell whiskey, but the race is on the uplift. Yet it has, in largest measure, to do the working out of its own fate and destiny. Anderson Locklear two years ago went to Washington, had an audience with the President and was told by the latter of his appreciation of Locklear's invitation to visit North Carolina and Roanoke island, the original

home of his people, Indians and whites.   The President
said that the history of the Croatans greatly interested
him.

It is found that the Croatans have, to a remarkable
degree, that sense of direction which is peculiar to all the
types of Indians and which is so acute as to be almost an
instinct.   Several of their people spoke about their use of
cross bows, and so far as can be ascertained they were
the only Indians in this country who used these weapons, which originated on the other side of the Atlantic,
and which the English used up to the time of Sir Walter
Raleigh.

Justice is but too often spoken of as tardy, and surely
the case of the Croatan Indians of North Carolina is one
which proves the   accuracy of this general statement.
It required three hundred years for them to come to
their own again, the descendents of the "Lost Colony of
Roanoke", and of these Indians on the North Carolina
coast who were described by the historians of the 1587
expedition by the English to these shores as a very noble,
well-favored and splendidly formed people, as indeed is
shown by the water-color drawing made by John
White, the artist of this noted expedition sent out
by that prince of exploiters, Sir Walter Raleigh, which
landed at Roanoke Island.   It is strange, but true, that
the writer made the first printed suggestion that the Croatan Indians of to-day are the descendents of Governor
White's "Lost Colony", this suggestion having been
made July 31st, 1885, though the idea had been advanced
by Mr. Hamilton McMillan, of Robeson county, North
Carolina, who has spent much of his life in the country
of the Croatans and who knows more of their history
and tradition than any other living man.   It was in 1887,

while a member of the North Carolina Legislature, that
Mr. McMillan advanced the idea and it was through his
personal influence with that body that this tribe was
given recognition.   In 1888 he embodied his opinions in
a brochure which advanced internal evidence and tradition with historical evidence in favor of the survival
of the "Lost Colony" in the persons of the Croatans of
this day.

*   *   *   *   *   *   *

RALEIGH'S FIRST EXPEDITION.

There was in 1584 the first expedition, under Raleigh's auspices, which landed on the North Carolina
coast, passed through an inlet and found the isle of
Roanoke, the largest in North Carolina with a fortified
village, the people being declared by these first explorers to be "gentle, loving and faithful, void of all guile
and treason and such as live after the manner of the
golden age".   These first English explorers, since they
could not be called colonists, remained here only two
months, had friendly relations with the Indians and
spent all their time making explorations but made no
effort to effect a settlement, returning to England and
carrying with them two natives, both chiefs, Manteo and
Wanchese, who received great attention in England and
who were brought back by the next expedition.   Manteo remaining to the last the good friend of the white
men while Manchese became their unlenting enemy.
The accounts of the Englishmen took back of this new
world, which Raleigh named "Virginia" in honor of the
so-called Virgin Queen Elizabeth, set England in a
flame, and bold adventurers rallied for a new journey,
the expedition sailing early in 1585, Sir Richard Gren-

ville. Raleigh's cousin, commanding. Virginia was the general name given all the territory which the English claimed on the basis of all discoveries, but it seems that there were two provinces, one called Carolana and the other Carolina, these adjoining. but Carolana soon went out of existence, if indeed it really existed, and the name Carolina covered all the territory within the charter of 1663, this being presently divided so that in 1719 the governments of North Carolina and South Carolina were made entirely distinct.   In the second expedition which Raleigh sent over were some of the greatest minds of that great age, including Thomas Chavendish, Thomas Hariot, John White, Phillip Amadas, who had been on the former expedition, and Ralph Lane. Grenville, high-tempered always though brave as a lion, burned a town of the Indians and destroyed their corn crop because one of them had stolen a silver cup.   This act was to bear fruit which soon brought woe to the white men. Grenville set a colony on Roanoke Island with Lane as Governor and in the late summer returned to England. He and Lane had had hot disputes on the outward voyage and Lane seems to have been aware that no good was intended.   The colony spent much time in exploration, and it is remarkable how much of the territory of the new world it visited.   It went up into what is now Virginia, near what is now Norfolk, explored the Roanoke river, which the natives called Moratoke, this indeed being the meaning for many years.   This time the natives were unfriendly and there was fighting during several of the expeditions   The white men had depended upon the natives for food, this being usually hominy, made from Indian corn, potatoes and various other roots, fish and game.   Hunger pressed so close that this colony had a council on one of its expeditions, but the explorers showed their bravery by deciding to persevere as long as half a pint of corn was left to the man.

They lived on any sort of food, even on the meat of dogs, and almost starved, as they had no seed corn, the Indians refusing to furnish it, and also planning to starve the English to death by going away and leaving all their planting grounds on the island of Roanoke unsown. The English had no skill in catching fish with weirs, which the Indians used to a great extent. The Indians formed a league against the whites who were on short commons and who had to watch day and night to guard against massacre. Governor Lane held as a hostage, one of the princes, Skyco by name, and treated him most kindly, and this kindness bore fruit, for he betrayed the Indian plot to massacre every settler, the English acting instantly, notifying their would-be murderers that they desired a grand council on the mainland, going there well armed and putting the then king and the chief conspiritors to death. The colonists then seized a good supply of corn and planted enough to last them two years, but suddenly Sir Francis Drake appeared with a great fleet of 23 vessels, offering to give the Englishmen food, ammunition, clothing and boats, and men for the latter. This generous offer was accepted but a great storm scattered the fleet and everything became gloomy in the extreme. Sir Richard Grenville had promised to come over but there was no sign of him and so the colonists, in the lowest spirits, decided to go home with Drake. There had been 108 of them but over a dozen had been killed or died. This was the sad end of the first actual English settlement in what is now the terri-

tory of the United States.   Directly after Lane left
Roanoke a ship which Raleigh had fitted out and provided with all necessaries arrived there and looked for
the colonists but found them not and two weeks later
Grenville came with three ships and also explored the
country fruitlessly.   He was so anxious to retain possession of it for England that he made the bold venture
of leaving 15 men behind him on Roanoke island pro-
viding these with full supplies and plenty of arms.   Englishmen saw the 15 no more, for when a year later
John White came over he was told by the savages that
these men had either been killed by the Indians or
drowed· while trying to go from Roanoke island to Croatan.

COLONISTS LIKED COUNTRY.

The colonists were charmed with the country, finding
grapes very sweet and large; papatour, which is now
known as Indian corn; opernauk, the native name for
the potato now known as the Irish potato, and the uppo-
woc, or tobacco. which was so much affected by the
Indian and which made itself a wonder among the Englishmen at once on both side of the ocean.   In 1587 Sir
Walter Raleigh, with his usual perseverance, made ready
a new colony, made John White the Governor with 12
assistants. who were virtually named as alderman, of
what was to be the "City of Raleigh in Virginia".   This
colony numbering 117, of whom 17 were women, 10 of
these accompanying their husbands.   Roanoke has
really a very poor harbor and Raleigh told his people
to make their home on the Chesapeak bay, to which one
party of Governor Lane's explorers had gone, but this
step was not taken.   It was the 22nd of July when the
little fleet reached this coast and Governor White at

The above illustration shows the photographs of three typical
Croatan Indians. Reading from left to right they are — Evander
Lowrie, Sias Locklear and Rev. Gilbert Locklear. The last named
is very erect and shows many of the characteristics of the typical
Indian. He is one of their leading ministers.

once started to Roanoke island. White had been with
Grenville on the 1585 expedition. He was one of the
best artists of his time and made very beautiful and ex-
act pictures of the natives, as well as the fauna and
flora of the new country, these being shown to Raleigh
and aiding much in developing interest in the work of
colonization. In 1590 they were engraved on copper
and printed in a number of languages by Theodore
DeBray, the chief German artist and printer of that
time. White was of pacific temper and his purpose was
to be friendly to the Indians. As soon as his boat had
pushed off from the ship he said that the sailors in the
latter had been directed not to take back to England
any of the planters, but to leave them on the island. It
was three days before the planters arrived, and they,
sturdy men and women, prepared to make their home
on the island. On the 13th of August, 1587, Manteo,
who remained the faithful friend of the Indians was
baptized by a clergyman of the established Church and
was made Lord of Roanoke and Dassamonguepeuk, this
being the only title of nobility ever given to a native of
the new world by English authorization. Five days after this baptism Governor White's daughter, Eleanor
Dare, the wife of Ananias Dare, one of the assistants,
gave birth to a daughter who was christened "Virginia",
and who was the first child of English parentage born
in this hemisphere. The colonists found they needed
many things, in spite of what was thought to be of ample provision for them, and they by vote decided that
White, their Governor, should go home as an agent for
all, so as to supply every need.

RALEIGH'S TROUBLES.

He sailed nine days after his baby granddaughter had been baptized and his eyes were the last which saw the ill-fated colonists.   England was then in a stir.   The great fight against Roman Catholic Spain was on and the country needed every man to do his duty.   With wonderful perseverence, in the midst of all the terrors of the time, Raleigh found means to send White back to Virginia in 1588.   He sailed in April with fifteen more planters and bountiful supplies but his vessels met war vessels of France and one of them was boarded and plundered.   Both vessels returned to England.   This was the last effort that year to help the Roanoke colonists, and it was in February, 1591, that White through Raleigh's influence, started for Virginia.   The commander of his little fleet thought more of plundering the Spaniards and the French than of the new colony and so it was August before the latter was reached.   Heavy storms came on and seven of the best men were lost by the capsizing of a boat in trying to reach Roanoke island.   One of the paintings made by White in 1585 showed a small boat sailing towards that island, in its bow standing a man holding aloft the cross.   On this relief visit White went personally in a boat and after a trying journey anchored at night in a little bay near the fort which had been built for the colonists; gave a call upon the trumpets and also a number of familiar English airs, but there was no answer.   When daylight came the party landed and saw on the shore, cut on a pine tree, "CRO," advanced towards the fort, found all the houses removed and all the place enclosed with a palisade of tree trunks of large size.   Within the little

fortress they found pig iron and lead; iron guns, cannon
shot and other heavy articles scattered here and there,
overgrown with grass, chests dug up their contents
scattered around.   White's own books being rotten from
the rain and his armor nearly destroyed by rust.   On
one of the gate posts at the entrance to the fort on a
great pine five feet above the ground, in large letters,
was deeply cut the word "Croatan".   There was not
another sign.   White, disheartened at this vanishing of
his colony, went back to his fleet and pleaded with the
captain in command to carry him to Croatan, which the
latter agreed to do, but delayed day after day, then declared his supplies were too short and sailed away to
the West Indies.   Such was White's farewell to his colony, his daughter and his grandchild.   This was the
fifth and last voyage of White, for it seems he remained
one whole year there and this makes it very probable
he was in the first expedition of 1584.

OBLIVION FALLS LIKE A PALL.

Oblivion fell like a pall upon the colony and it came
to be known through all the years as "The Lost Colony
of Roanoke".   Time was to lift the curtain and let in the
light.   The Anglo-Saxons have ever had a deep-seated
antipathy towards intermarriage with people of another
color, whether it be brown, black or yellow.   The French,
less squeamish in these matters, began at a very early day
to foster such intermarriages, and this was one of the
factors which brought about the influence the French
had with their Indian allies.   As a matter of fact the Indians, as the whites found them, certainly in this part of
the world, were a seemly people, as the well executed
pictures by John White, (the originals of which, in color,

are in the British Museum, the United States and the
State of North Carolina having duplicates,) show clearly
that both the Indian men and women were comely to a
very remarkable degree and the various work they did
showed if not civilization, something which bordered
upon it. To tell the truth it has always been the whites
who have brought upon themselves the Indian hatred
and revenge and whether it be in Peru, Mexico or the
United States this has been over and over again the
case. Yet as to these lost colonists and the Indians with
whom they were taken to Croatan there must have been
intermarriage. Many things go to prove this, among
them being the radical characteristics of the Croatan Indians, who are now in several counties south of Raleigh,
the capital of the State and at least 200 miles in an air
line from Roanoke Island.   There are blendings of the
Indian race and that of the Englishmen; the hair, eyes,
etc., showing the influence of the English strain.   Croatan or Croatoan was southward from Roanoke Island
and directly upon the coast, and it was very near the
old town of Beaufort, in Carteret county, one of the oldest maps date 1666, showing it under this name.   The
sound directly west of Roanoke Island still bears the
name of Croatan.   Some historians think the name of the
tribe as Croatan and of their island Croatan.   Really it is
not an island at all but one of those long strips of sand known
as "banks", which are barriers between the ocean and the
chain of North Carolina sounds.   The Indians called
their own territory Dasamonguepeuk.   The name Croatoan carved upon the great post of the palisade at Fort
Raleigh was placed according to secret understanding
between Governor White and his colonists to designate
the place to which the latter had gone, in case they left

the island.   White knew Croatan was an island southward from Roanoke because he said Manteo and the
friendly savages of Roanoke Island were born there.
When John Lawson the first real historian of North Carolina, visited this section in 1708 he said the Hatteras
Indians who lived at Roanoke Island or much frequented
it told him several of their ancestors were white people
and "could talk in a book" as Lawson did; that he saw
frequently grey eyes among those Indians and among no
other tribes, and that they valued themselves extremely
for their kinship to the English and showed readiness to
do the most friendly offices for them.   So then the Croatans were the Hatorask or Hatteras Indians.

It was in 1730 that Scotchmen arrived in the section
of the State where the Croatans now are and at the coming of these their records show that they found on Lumber river, Robeson county, a large tribe of Indians speaking English, farming, owning slaves and showing many
evidences of civilization.   These held their lands in common and land titles became known only after the advent
of the whites,   The first grant to any of the Croatans is
dated in 1732, being to Henry Berry and James Lowrie,
two of the leading men, and covered large tracts in Robeson county.   The Croatans were found to be hospitable
and entirely friendly to their white neighbors.   After
the white settlers began to come in a part of this tribe
went north and settled around the Great Lakes, some of
their descendants now being in Canada, west of Lake
Ontario, while a number of these people, described as
whites, emigrated into the great North Carolina mountain region, the tribe in Robeson county now claiming
certain families in western North Carolina to be, like
themselves, descendenants of the lost English colonists.

When the first whites arrived Indians had built excellent
roads connecting their most distant settements with the
principle seat of their government, if so it can be called,
which was on the Lumbee river, that being the Indian name of what is now termed the Lumber river.
One of these roads extends for twenty miles to what is
called Fayetteville, and their greatest highway yet bears
the name of the "Lowrie road", and is used to this day,
extending from Fayetteville through two counties to an
old settlement on the Pee Dee river.

Many men of this tribe of Croatans served in the Con-
tinental army during the war of the revolution and a
number during the war of 1812.   Until the year 1835
they were allowed to vote and to perform militia duty,
owned slaves, built churches and school houses and
lived comfortably, many of them after the English manner, but a State convention which met that year denied
the right to vote to all "free persons of color".   After
their disfranchisement in 1835 the Indians, who rebelled
against being classed as mulattoes, became suspicious of
the whites and it was very difficult to get any information from them regarding their history, though of traditions they had no end.   The first real investigator was
Hamilton McMillan, and strange to say his investigation
was due to an incident during the civil war.   One of the
greatest of all the families of the tribe is the Lowries and
three young men of this tribe, instead of being sent to the
front as soldiers, were treated as colored persons, drafted
and sent to work to build Fort Fisher, the great defense
below Wilmington.   While they were being taken there
by a white soldier they were killed by him, it was believed.   There was an inquest and when it was ended
George Lowery, an aged Indian, made an address to a

concourse of his people in which he said they had always been friends of the white men, that they were free
long before the white men ever came to America and
had in fact always been free; that they lived in Roanoke, Virginia, and that when the English came there
the tribe treated them kindly; that one of the tribe was
taken to England on an English vessel and saw that
country; that the tribe had always been friendly with
the white men and taken the English to live with them
and that in their veins was the blood of white men as
well as Indian, and that in order to be great like the
English they had taken the white man's language and
religion, for they had been told they would prosper if
they would adopt the white men's ways. Lowery said
further on that in the wars between white men and Indians his people had always fought on the side of the white
men; that they had moved to the section where they
now were and fought for liberty for the white men, yet
the latter had treated them as negroes and in this case
had shot down their young men and given no justice
and this in a land where the Croatans had been always
free.

MR. M'MILLAN'S RESEARCHES.

Hamilton McMillan began his investigations in the
most critical manner in 1875, when his home was in the
centre of the Croatan settlement, where he had the best
opportunities of interviewing leading men of the tribe.
The first step was to find the reason for the striking English names found among the Croatans, and so these
were compared with those on the roll of white's lost colony. Out of the 120 persons in that colony 90 family
names were represented and of these White, Bailey,
Dare, Cooper, Stevens, Sampson, Harvie, Howe, John-

son, Willes, Brown, Smith, Harris, Little, Taylor, Jones,
Brooks, Coleman, Graham, Bennett, Lucas, Wilkinson,
Vicars, Berry, Butler, Wright, Allen, Chapman, Lasie,
Cheven, Paiue, Scott, Little, Martin, Patterson, Bridger,
Wood, Powell, Pierce, Charman, Payne and Sampson
are found among the Croatans of this time. The name
Darr, Durr and Dorr is variously used by these people
and is really Dare. Their pronunciation is broad and
they use great numbers of old English words. Families
bearing the names Dorr or Durr are to be found in the
western part of North Carolina and these are claimed by
the Croatans, who assert that the Dares, Coopers, Har-
vies and a few others retain the purity of blood and
were generally the pioneers of immigration.

They have a tradition of their leader or chief who
went to England but have not preserved his name,
speaking of him as Mayno or Maynor, but a woman
of great age spoke of their head man as Wanoake, which
may be a corruption of Roanoke.

The name Mayno is quite common among them and
represents in their tongue a quiet and law-abiding people.

The great difficulty has been to ascertain the date
when the Croatans left the coast country for the interior, but it seems certain that they have lived in
Robeson county over 220 years. The traditions
universal among them show they were seated there
long before the great war with the Tuscaroras began in
1711. It seems that in their friendship for the whites,
some of the Croatans fought under Colonel Branwell,
who was in command of the troops and friendly Indians
sent up from South Carolina to aid the North Carolina settlers in crushing the Tuscaroras after the great

massacre by the latter.   The tradition goes further that the Croatans in this war had taken a number of Matta-muskett Indians prisoners and took the latter back with them to Robeson as slaves, the decendants of these Mattamusketts yet living there and claiming this decent, some of them being able to locate the region where their ancestors lived.   It is to be noticed that the Croatans always speak of "Virginia" as he place where their people lived.   They mean the Virginia of Sir Walter Raleigh's founding.

TARDY JUSTICE.

The tardy justice which North Carolina gave to these strange and most interesting people came to them in the spring of 1885, and when the act of the Legislature recognizing them as Croatan Indians was publicly read, an aged Indian, a very intelligent man, remarked that he had always heard his ancestors called Hatteras Indians. There are those who believe that the settlement on the Lumber river was made as early as 1650, for French Huguenots, exiled from their homes, who found refuge in South Carolina, sent certain of their number as settlers to North Carolina in 1709 and these found the Croatans with good farms and roads and evidently long settled there.

The language spoken by the Croatans is a very pure but quaint old Anglo-Saxon and there are in daily use some 75 words which have come down from the great days of Raleigh and his mighty mistress, Queen Elizabeth.   These old Saxon words arrest attention instantly.   For man they say "mon," pronounce "father" "feyther;" use mension for measurement; ax for ask; hosen for hose; lovend for loving; wit for knowledge;

housen for houses. Many of the words in daily use by
them have for many a long year been entirely absolete
in English speaking countries. Their homes have always been neat in the extreme and they are very hospitable to strangers and always ready to befriend white
people. They are intensely proud and boast alike of
their English and their Indian ancestors and blood.
While their disposition is peaceable they will fight des-
perately when aroused. They are shy as a race, though
under the new conditions and in the more Catholic
spirit which now prevails they are coming into the
open. Their life has been away from crowds of other
races and their homes away from the public roads.
Some of them now show their Indian traits even more
strongly than they did a century ago. Their English
love for good roads is shown by the fact that they have
been and yet are great road builders and have always
had the best public roads in the State. No special census has been taken of them, but the number is said to be
not less than 5,000, of which more than half are in Robeson
county. There are about 1,500 children of school age,
of these the roll having been made. The State has provided a separate normal school for these people; the
Governor has addessed them; they are being aroused
to fresh pride in their ancestry and in learning and their
development is becoming rapid. The Legislature took
every step to safeguard these people and amended the
general law by declaring null and void any and all
marriages between Croatan Indians and persons of
negro decent to the third generation inclusive.

They are quick-witted people. One of them was ex-
United States Senator Revels, of Mississippi, who was
classed as a mulatto while really a Croatan who

was born in Robeson county.   The Croatans are almost
universally owners of land and in Robeson county thus
occupy a territory of more than 60,000 acres, all owned
by them.   They are now beginning themselves to look
more closely into traditions and some of their leaders
state that the traditions of every family which bears the
name of one of the lost colonists point to the Roanoke
country as that of their ancestors, it being a further tradition that long after they left the coast country and
went into the interior they held communication with
the poople on the coast and it may have been some of
these very up country Croatans, visiting their former
home, who were seen by Lawson in 1708 and who spoke
of their ancestors as persons who could "talk in a book".
Early French, English, Irish and German immigrants
who came among the Croatans in the Robeson section
seem to have frequently married these Indians.   The
name Chavis, now common, is a corruption of a French
name, as also Blaux, while Leary was O'Leary.   In
building they show much skill.   They have the Indian
love for bright colors and when walking in bodies they
march in Indian file, one behind the other.   They
brought with them from the coast country the love of
tobacco and the knowledge of how to grow it and the
earliest visitors to the Robeson section found patches of
tobacco near their houses.   They never forget an obli-
gation or a debt, nor do they forget a kindness or an insult.   A century ago they had good inns for travelers.
Their women are extremely handsome and the most
noted one among them now is Rhoda Lowrie, the widow of Henry Berry Lowrie, a famous outlaw.   State
Auditor Dixon recently visited the Croatans and spoke
to a great assemblage of them at Pates, the location of

their normal college.   There he saw Rhoda, who used to be a great beauty.   Her husband's father and several other Croatans, not recognized then as whites or Indians, but as negroes, when sent to work during the civil war on the forts, left and went home, were pursued by the Home Guard and several were shot, being classed as deserters.   Henry Berry Lowrie was then only a youth, but he swore by the blood of his ancestors that he would kill every one of the Home Guard who had shot his father.   He kept this terrible oath to the letter, except in the case of one of the Home Guard, who fled the State to escape the swift and sure death which had come to his comrades.   Lowrie associated with himself other daring spirits and it required State militia and even Federal troops to crush out what came to be known as the "Lowrie outlaws".   Their leader accidentally killed himself with his gun; his brother, Steve, for whom a reward, of $5,000 was offered by the State, was shot from ambush, and the trouble was quelled, but not before many a white man had been killed, and a reign of terror existed which attracted national attention and brought about action by the President and the War Department.

INFLUENCE OF ENGLISH.

The dominating influence of the English upon this race has been shown very clearly by the language and by the customs, which have retained nothing of the savage.   There are no Indian words in use, nor have there been these hundred years or more, and there are no Indian customs.   The Indian is shown, however, in some of the facial characteristics, in the physique, and in the walk, the latter having much of the red man's

stride and swing, which when once seen is not to be forgotten. The carriage of the women is superb, and
they unconsciously look like statues in some of their
poses. Their color is very rich, their figure ample and
graceful in every outline.

Of course there are doubters and among historians,
too, as to the status of these people, and there are those
who believe that they are a mixture or blend of the first
white settlers who it is claimed pushed up into that region from Charleston, S. C., and the Indians of that locality. A comparison of the typical Croatan and one of
the Roanoke Island Indians as painted with extreme
care by John White, Sir Walter Raleigh's great artist,
shows many points of resemblance between that race
and the present day Croatans, among whom splendid
figures are the rule rater than the exception.

ONE ARGUMENT AS TO RALEIGH'S COLONISTS.

The argument has been advanced by some that Raleigh's colonists when they left Roanoke Island, did not
go to the southward, but that they went to the northeast,
and that they fixed themselves about the point where
Avoca now is, in Bertie county, and that they there
built themselves substantial houses; that the Indians fell
upon them, under the leadership of Wanchese or some
of his friends, and massacred almost all, great rivers being on either side, which the colonists could not cross,
but that the Indians spared a few, including "a young
mayde"; that those captured were taken further up the
country and that the Englishmen of their number were
made to build houses, partly at least of stone, for their
Indian masters, and that it was these houses and these
captives of whom Captain John Smith heard and whom

he made note, the information concerning them having
been brought by Indian runners to him and his colonists
at Jamestown.   Those who hold this view that the colonists after leaving Roanoke Island went towards the
northwest and settled as above stated, say that Governor
White and other leaders had been up into that part of
the country and had fixed on this as a place better for
a settlement than Roanoke Island, which was and is extremely isolated and in a section subject to storms, there
being entirely open water all about.   To get to Avoca
the colonists had a very good boat, of sufficient size to
carry them.   Those who hold this view believe further
that the Indians with blue eyes and fair hair and ruddy
complexions who were seen by latter explorers on the
North Carolina coast were not the descendants of the
Lost Colony at all but of Indian women and of the first
party of Englishmen put ashore, the latter not being on
Roanoke Island, but on one of the long sand-banks between that island and the sea, which form a barrier between the sea and the sounds which have always marked
the North Carolina coast.

EVIDENCE OF RELICS.

There has recently been found in Robeson county, in
the heart of the Croatan settlement, an iron tomahawk,
such as were described by Col. William Byrd as sold
along the great Indian "trading path" and along the
"Lowery Road" by traders early in the eighteenth century.   Another find is an ancient cross-bow of the English make and model, of the type which was still used
in Queen Elizabeth's time.   This bow bears the marks of
much use.   A hand-mill of the most primitive type, but

showing very clearly its English origin, has also been
found in one of the Croatan houses, with the tradition
that it had been used by their people before they moved
from the coast country.   There are a number of Croatans in the county of Cumberland and there was a stone
church near the present village of Hope Mills.   The
church itself is gone, but the foundation of brown stone
can be seen plainly.

Thus linked together the history of the Lost Colony of
Roanoke and that of the most interesting of Indians on
this continent; interesting because in the blending of
their English blood there comes down through the cen-
turies so much of the old world and the new; of the
great Raleigh, the master spirit of his age, and of the
Indians along this coast, who seem to have been models
of their race; a strange linking of those first baptisms of
the baby white girl and the Indian king, and of the new
awakening of education and hope and pride among the
Croatans, to whom North Carolina at last holds out the
hand of recognition.

Do You Want to Buy a Home

———————— OR AN ————————

INSURANCE POLICY?

IF SO APPLY TO THE UNDERSIGNED

THE LaFAYETTE MUTUAL LIFE INSURANCE CO.
FAYETTEVILLE, N. C.

Offers the best opportunity to make good for the whole
community above any other institution in existence. The
Company commenced business on July 4th, 1909, and has
at the present time over 400 policies in force. The Company has assets for the protection of its policy-holders to
an amount in excess of $10,000.00.

The management of this company is the most economical of
any Life Insurance Company ever organized. As an evidence of this fact the Company has already over $1,000.00
earned surplus, belonging to the policy-holders.

For further information write, phone, or telegraph

E. E. PAGE, Supt. of Agents,
LUMBERTON, N. C.

Price 50 Cts.

FREEMAN PRINTING COMPANY
LUMBERTON, N. C

Lightning Source UK Ltd.
Milton Keynes UK
UKHW040431110820
368039UK00001B/243

9 789354 042942